Dear Kate,
Enjoy!
love,
Anna

December 25, 2002

glorious gifts
from the garden

glorious gifts

from the garden

inspirational projects from the potting shed

STEPHANIE DONALDSON   PHOTOGRAPHY BY MICHELLE GARRETT

LORENZ BOOKS

DEDICATION
To my long-suffering children Andrew and Charlotte, who went without their summer holiday so that I could write this book. Thank you.

THIS EDITION PUBLISHED BY LORENZ BOOKS IN 2002

© ANNESS PUBLISHING LIMITED 1997, 2002

LORENZ BOOKS IS AN IMPRINT OF ANNESS PUBLISHING LIMITED
HERMES HOUSE, 88–89 BLACKFRIARS ROAD, LONDON SE1 8HA

PUBLISHED IN THE USA BY LORENZ BOOKS, ANNESS PUBLISHING INC.
27 WEST 20TH STREET, NEW YORK, NY 10011

WWW.LORENZBOOKS.COM

THIS EDITION DISTRIBUTED IN CANADA BY GENERAL PUBLISHING
895 DON MILLS ROAD, 400-402 PARK CENTRE,
TORONTO, ONTARIO M3C 1W3 TEL: 416 445 3333 FAX: 416 445 5991

A CIP CATALOGUE RECORD FOR THIS BOOK IS AVAILABLE FROM THE BRITISH LIBRARY.

PUBLISHER: JOANNA LORENZ
SENIOR EDITOR: LINDSAY PORTER
DESIGNER: NIGEL PARTRIDGE
PHOTOGRAPHER: MICHELLE GARRETT
STYLISTS: MICHELLE GARRETT AND STEPHANIE DONALDSON

PREVIOUSLY PUBLISHED AS *FROM THE POTTING SHED*

1 3 5 7 9 10 8 6 4 2

Contents

INTRODUCTION

The potting shed is the gardener's refuge. A place to be or to do according to inclination – where "ought to" and "should" become unimportant and the pleasure of pottering is paramount. Close the door behind you and enjoy the time to work unhurried, at nature's pace.

In spite of its utilitarian name, the potting shed is far more than a useful storage area and behind-the-scenes workroom for the gardener's *al fresco* performance. For many gardeners, it is a rustic refuge from everyday concerns, a quiet and solitary place for contemplation and gentle activity, which may or may not be of a horticultural nature.

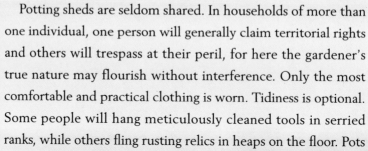

Potting sheds are seldom shared. In households of more than one individual, one person will generally claim territorial rights and others will trespass at their peril, for here the gardener's true nature may flourish without interference. Only the most comfortable and practical clothing is worn. Tidiness is optional. Some people will hang meticulously cleaned tools in serried ranks, while others fling rusting relics in heaps on the floor. Pots may be carefully cleaned and sorted ready for use or left where last discarded, according to inclination. Compost is neatly sacked and stacked or thrown with abandon over every surface. Most of us come somewhere between the two extremes, for while

Top: The gardener's tools find a home in the potting shed.
ABOVE LEFT: Garden flowers are casually displayed in a treasured jug.
RIGHT: Stencils adorn a galvanized tin bucket.

8

we admire orderliness, a natural impatience engenders a tendency towards disorder, and in this one area of our lives, we feel completely free to be exactly what we are – occasionally tidy and well organized, but rather more often not.

For many of us, our garden is our only real connection with the uncontrollable natural world – with the vagaries of climate, the variability of soil, the vigour of weeds and the voracity of pests. While the garden holds as many disappointments as delights, the potting shed is full of hopeful dreams. The seeds we sow flourish in our imagination, and bulbs pierce the soil like well-rehearsed synchronized swimmers, with never a shoot too premature or tardy. Of course we know differently, but each year we entertain the possibility that maybe this year will be the one when our dreams come true.

There is a world of creative possibilities in all aspects of gardening, and while not all the projects in this book are dependent on the ownership of a potting shed, all have been inspired by a love of gardening and many happy hours spent pottering in a shed, conservatory or kitchen. Some projects involve sawing, some stitching and others painting, but all of them are intended to be

enjoyed by the gardener or used in the garden.

It is hoped that these projects will provide gardeners with the inspiration to disappear down to the end of the garden, and revel in the pleasure of a productive afternoon's activity in the potting shed.

ABOVE RIGHT AND LEFT: Tools of the trade evoke the pleasures of pottering.
ABOVE LEFT: The vision of a flourishing border has its origins in hours whiled away in the potting shed.

USEFUL MATERIALS

The potting shed is not usually considered to be the realm of the expert with extensive experience and a large armoury of well-honed tools, copious quantities of nails and screws already sorted into the correct sizes and a comprehensive selection of seasoned timber. This is the world of the relaxed amateur, who will improvise when the suggested material is not available, will substitute nails for screws without feeling shame, will devise colour schemes from half-used tins of paint and as a result will bring a quirky individuality to the product of their endeavours, which often has far more charm than the object they initially intended to make.

Most of the projects in this book can be made with a minimum of tools and with materials readily available from DIY outlets, garden centres and art shops. In the few instances

LEFT: Spare pots of paint left over from larger jobs can be used to create other colour schemes.

where specialist materials have been used, they have been sourced to ensure that they are obtainable in small quantities by mail order or from specialist suppliers.

The majority of the projects are decorative and do not involve much in the way of carpentry or other specialist crafts. Many stores now sell simple rough wooden boxes and unpainted tinware, while garden centres have a huge range of terracotta pots, watering cans and rustic bird-houses. These items can be bought inexpensively for use in some of the projects and transformed

BELOW: Tools need not be ordered and indexed; pots and buckets can be used to store the gardener's paraphernalia until needed.

ABOVE: Many paints are produced in "historic" colours that have a subtle depth of hue suited to the garden.

with a variety of decorative techniques. It isn't always necessary to have a project in mind when buying as a stock of "useful" boxes, tins and bits and pieces is essential equipment in the potting shed. When the mood strikes, the last thing you will want to do is go shopping before you can start pottering.

Junk shops are a rich source of all kinds of materials – old terracotta pots, watering cans, buckets, old seed trays, trugs and garden tools are all worth looking out for. Even if you don't get round to doing anything with them, the collection will add character to the shed.

There is a limit to improvization with tools and it is advisable to keep a basic tool kit, which might comprise the following: tenon saw, large and small claw hammers, small wooden mallet, pliers, selection of screwdrivers, electric drill, staple gun, selection of nails and screws, PVA glue.

RIGHT: Old tools add character to the shed and can often be found in junk shops.

You will also find it useful to have two or three gauges of galvanized and plastic-coated wire, some plant labels and a variety of garden strings.

It was Thoreau who said, "Beware of all enterprises that require new clothes", and in this instance you may be assured that he would thoroughly approve of the old favourites which are recommended shed-wear.

THE GARDENER

Gift ideas for and from the gardener, from useful equipment to decorative accessories, including lotions and potions to protect the skin and soothe and care for tired muscles.

We have been gardeners since Adam and Eve cultivated Eden, and although for many of us gardening is now more a leisure activity than a necessity, the instinct to till and sow remains deep within us.

Many of us begin a love affair with the garden during childhood, often following the horticultural example of a parent or grandparent. We learn the patience required for gardening by planting a peach stone or apple pip and waiting for the tree to grow, or by making a first garden border planted with colourful flowers. We may help in the vegetable garden or flower borders, learning names and techniques and gaining experience without even being aware that we have become gardeners' apprentices. This childhood apprenticeship is a very valuable experience and will serve us each time we start afresh with a new garden.

Top: A few well-worn tools are the hallmark of the passionate gardener.
Above left and right: Growing and harvesting your own produce brings many rewards.

It isn't necessary to come to gardening in childhood, however, to become passionate about it. Its pleasures and pitfalls can be happened upon at any stage of life. One of the joys of meeting new and enthusiastic gardeners of whatever age is to observe their

wonder at having grown something from a seed or successfully rooted a cutting. These little miracles are an everyday part of life, which we only encounter when we learn to garden. For us gardeners, regularly getting our hands into the soil, "earthing" ourselves, is an essential part of life and renews our contact with the natural world.

Any gardener will be able to tell you that caring for a garden and spending

time at work in the potting shed are valuable escape routes from the stresses and strains that plague modern life, but they can also be physically tiring activities that leave the gardener in need of a little luxurious pampering at the end of a busy day. In this section, there are projects to soothe and care for the hard-working gardener. Projects include a hand-care kit and relaxing herbal bath, as well as a collection of practical and attractive ideas for garden gifts, from a first aid kit specifically designed to suit the needs of the gardener, to a decorated apron

Top: Freshly dug potatoes and beetroot nestle in a hand-painted trug.

Above left: Peat pots await this season's planting.

15

GARDENER'S APRON

If you are the sort of gardener who likes to nip out into the garden for ten minutes or so, in between other tasks, then this gardener's apron will prove an ideal garment. With pockets filled and rings loaded with useful tools and materials, there is everything at hand for a productive potter without ruining your clothes or wasting precious minutes locating gloves, secateurs, string or raffia. The apron can be made from scratch or the "flowerpot" pockets and brass rings can be added to a ready-made apron. Either way, you will be ready to garden at a moment's notice.

MATERIALS AND EQUIPMENT
TO MAKE THE APRON FROM SCRATCH:
old apron
newspaper
pencil
dressmaker's pins
1 m (1 yd) dark green sailcloth
scissors
cotton thread: dark green and beige
sewing machine
5 m (5 yd) beige woven tape
tape measure
30 cm (12 in) natural hessian
needle
8 2.5 cm (1 in) brass rings
TO ADD POCKETS TO A
READY-MADE APRON:
newspaper
pencil
tape measure
30 cm (12 in) natural hessian
dressmaker's pins
scissors
sewing machine
beige cotton thread
3 m (3 yd) beige woven tape
needle
8 2.5 cm (1 in) brass rings

ABOVE: *The flowerpot pockets hold the gardener's essentials.*

1 Fold the old apron in half vertically, lay it on the newspaper and draw around it, adding a 1 cm (½ in) allowance. Cut out the pattern, pin it onto the sailcloth and cut around the pattern.

2 Hem around the apron with green cotton thread. Cut three x 60 cm (24 in) lengths of tape.

3 Using beige cotton thread, attach one length at the neck and the other two at each side.

4 Cut two paper patterns for the pockets following the templates at the back of the book.

5 Lay the paper patterns on the hessian, pin in place and cut out one small and two large pockets.

6 Fold over a 2 cm (¾ in) seam allowance and pin in place.

7 Zigzag stitch all around each pocket to prevent fraying. Cut a piece of beige woven tape 19 cm (7½ in) long. Turn under a 1 cm (½ in) seam allowance at each end and stitch in place.

8 Pin the tape to the top edge of the small top pocket to make the "rim". It should overlap slightly at each end. Turn under a 1 cm (½ in) seam allowance and stitch in place.

9 Cut four 25 cm (10 in) lengths of tape. Pin two pieces of tape to the top edge of each of the large pockets to make the rim. They should overlap slightly at each end. Turn under a 1 cm (½ in) seam allowance and stitch.

10 Cut eight 10 cm (4 in) lengths of tape. Thread a brass ring onto each piece, turn over 2 cm (¾ in) of tape and stitch to secure the ring.

11 Pin the taped rings to the rims of the pockets, so that the rings are positioned just above the lower edge of the rim. Stitch close to the upper rim. Sew the flowerpot pockets onto the apron using beige thread.

GARDENER'S HAND-CARE KIT

Working in the garden is wonderfully therapeutic and excellent exercise, but your hands can suffer, especially in cold or wet weather. Good gloves are invaluable, but inevitably there are tasks for which gloves are too cumbersome. This healing barrier cream can be used to protect the hands when applied before gardening and as a treatment for chapped hands or cuts and scratches. The camomile oil is soothing and excellent for chilblains, while the geranium oil helps wounds and scratches to heal quickly, controls inflammation and improves circulation and skin tone. The lemon oil softens hardened skin. Pack the cream in a box with a bar of soap, an absorbent towel, a pumice stone and a nailbrush, and the gardener will find everything needed to keep hands in tiptop condition.

MATERIALS AND EQUIPMENT
25 g (1 oz) lanolin
15 g (½ oz) white beeswax
double boiler
whisk
75 g (3 oz) almond oil
50 ml (2 fl oz) purified water
10 drops camomile oil
5 drops geranium oil
5 drops lemon oil
lidded container
wooden box
selection of hand-care items

3 Still whisking, add the water a few drops at a time. The mixture will very quickly emulsify into a thick cream.

4 Stir in the essential oils and pour into a lidded container. Pack the container in a wooden box with the gifts listed above.

1 Slowly melt the lanolin and beeswax in a double boiler.

2 Whisk the mixture, gradually adding the almond oil. The mixture will thicken slightly and become opaque.

RIGHT: *The home-made hand cream makes a very welcome gift when presented in a decorative pot along with other cleansing treats.*

HERBAL BATH

At the end of a busy day in the garden or potting shed, muscles may be tired and sometimes chilled. This is the perfect opportunity for a long hot soak in a bath scented with herbs to aid relaxation and reduce muscle tension. A mixture of equal parts of lavender, lime and camomile flowers is used, all of which help to relieve tension, while the lavender also releases its delicious fragrance into the water. Lemon balm, hops and passionflower could also be added, especially just before bed as they have a sedative effect. The herbal mixture is packed into little fabric bags, which can be floated in the bath or hung under a running tap. Window scrim, bought inexpensively from a hardware store, is used to make the bags. To preserve the aromatic and healing qualities of the herbs, store the bags in a sealed container. Each bag can be used three or four times. Squeeze it out after use and hang in a warm place to dry out completely.

MATERIALS AND INGREDIENTS
25 g (1 oz) lavender flowers
25 g (1 oz) lime flowers and leaves
25 g (1 oz) camomile flowers
6–8 fabric bags, 15 x 7.5 cm (6 x 3 in)
string

1 Weigh the flowers and mix together in a bowl.

2 Divide the mixture between the fabric bags and tie securely with string, forming a decorative bow.

LEFT: Garden twine and a plant label are used as decorative finishes and complete the gardening theme.

FIRST AID KIT

Too many minor garden injuries go untreated because the first aid kit is in the house and it is too much effort to take off muddy boots and other garden wear to treat a small cut or a painful thorn or splinter. These small injuries are often left untended until the garden tasks are finished, by which time infection may have set in. Fortunately, most injuries clear up quickly, but just occasionally something more serious develops. A first aid kit prepared specifically for the gardener would be welcome in any potting shed. A sturdy wooden or tin box with a snugly fitting lid should be used as the container. Conventionally a first aid kit is a white box with a red cross but in this instance the box is painted green to indicate its horticultural purpose. All the remedies included are herbal or homeopathic, but these can be replaced with conventional treatments.

MATERIALS AND EQUIPMENT
*wooden or tin box, approximately
25 x 20 cm (10 x 8 in)
green gloss or satin-finish paint
paintbrush
pencil
ruler
masking tape
red enamel paint
pack of surgical gloves (for when it is
difficult to wash hands)
scissors
tweezers (for splinters)
selection of waterproof plasters
2 sizes of stretch bandage
cotton wool
arnica cream (for bruises)
tea tree cream (antiseptic)
calendula cream (for sore, rough skin)
hypercal tincture (for cuts and
abrasions)
pyrethrum spray (for insect bites and
stings)
apis mel homeopathic tablets (for insect
bites and stings)*

1 Paint the box inside and out with green paint.

2 Draw a cross on the lid using a pencil and ruler. Mask around the cross and paint it with red enamel paint. It is less fiddly to mask either the vertical or horizontal arm first and then paint the other arm once the first is dry. Fill the box with some or all of the contents listed above.

LEFT: *Place the box in a prominent position in the shed and replenish stocks when necessary.*

GARDENER'S SCARF

Many a happy day's gardening has been ruined by the persistent presence of insects such as wasps, flies and midges. This colourful gardener's scarf has a little pocket sewn onto it to hold a sachet impregnated with essential oils with insect-repellent properties. Worn around the neck or tied around the brim of a hat, the scarf will keep the buzzing and biting insects at bay. A variety of oils are suitable; although citronella is the best known, it is more pungent than aromatic, and you may prefer to use lavender or peppermint oil or a mixture of lemon and clove or geranium and eucalyptus. If the scarf is a gift, a brightly coloured hessian bag can be made to hold the scarf along with a supply of sachets and a bottle of the essential oil. Include instructions for using the scarf and the sachets. If the scarf is kept folded in a plastic bag when not in use, the oils will remain effective for many months.

MATERIALS AND EQUIPMENT
*fabric, 50 x 50 cm (20 x 20 in), plus
20 x 10 cm (8 x 4 in) for pocket
dressmaker's pins
iron
sewing machine
matching thread
needle
4 pieces felt, 15 x 7.5 cm (6 x 3 in)
cotton wool or wadding
essential oil
hessian bag, 20 x 30 cm (8 x 12 in)*

1 Fold over a hem all around the fabric for the scarf. Pin in place, press with a hot iron and stitch the hem.

2 Fold over a hem on one edge of the fabric for the pocket and stitch.

3 Fold the pocket in half, pin the raw edges together and stitch. Turn the pocket right side out and press.

4 Pin the pocket onto one corner of the scarf and stitch in place.

5 Fold each felt piece in half and stuff with cotton wool or wadding impregnated with 6–10 drops of oil for each sachet. Pin around the edges and stitch securely.

RIGHT: Provide several of the oil-soaked sachets with the scarf.

NEW GARDENER'S GIFT SET

Long experience teaches the gardener which tools are absolutely essential. These are the ones which seldom become rusty and, if they do, must be renovated or replaced, while less useful tools languish at the back of the shed, too complicated to use or too difficult to clean – the horticultural equivalent of the pasta-making machine. The selection of tools in this gift set has been made from experience and would be very useful to a new gardener. It would, perhaps, be ideal as a house-warming present for a young couple about to tackle their first garden or as an appealing retirement gift for someone who has never previously had the time to garden.

ABOVE: With the right tools, new gardeners can begin to enjoy their own produce.

MATERIALS AND EQUIPMENT
*25 cm (10 in) terracotta pot
shredded wood or straw for packing
trowel
fork
dibber
weed lifter (optional)
secateurs
string
gloves
sisal string
label*

2 Push the tools and other equipment into the packing material so that they stand upright and give the appearance of growing out of the pot. If necessary, add more packing material to keep the tools in position.

3 For the finishing touch, tie a piece of sisal string around the pot and add a label to identify the giver.

1 Fill the pot with shredded wood or straw. Pack tightly to ensure it will support the tools in an upright position.

RIGHT: Favourite tools are used time and again, and are always kept to hand.

HERALD OF SPRING

Gardeners are always delighted to be given spring bulbs. If you are planning to give bulbs as a gift, order them well ahead of time or get down to the garden centre in mid-August for the best possible choice. To make this a really special gift, the bulbs are removed from their plastic bags and packed instead into hessian bags. These allow the bulbs to breathe and can be used to store them after flowering. A new wooden box is "weathered" by painting it with diluted liquid seaweed plant food, and the sacks of bulbs are stacked in the box with some terracotta pots to plant them in. Bulbs are not exclusively spring-flowering: a winter-flowering bulb collection could be made up of snowdrops, aconites, cyclamen and crocus; a summer bulb collection could include galtonia, crinum and a selection of alliums and lilies. Autumn-flowering bulbs such as crocosmia, colchicum, nerine and amaryllis would also make an unusual collection.

MATERIALS AND EQUIPMENT
3 pieces hessian, 60 x 45 cm
(24 x 18 in)
dressmaker's pins
sewing machine
matching cotton thread
3 bags of bulbs
scissors
stiff card
glue
hole punch
sisal string
wooden box, approximately 30 x 25 cm
(12 x 10 in)
seaweed plant food
paintbrush
3 terracotta pots

1 To make the sacks, fold each piece of hessian in half. Pin and stitch the side and base seams, using double seams if you want a more professional finish. Take the bulbs from their original packaging and place them in the sacks.

3 To attach the label to the bag, make a hole in the label using a hole punch and thread through a length of sisal string.

ABOVE: *Decorative labels indicate the contents of the bag. Cultivation instructions may be written on the back.*

2 Select a picture from the packaging to use as the label. Cut round it and mount it on stiff card, then cut carefully around the image.

4 To "weather" the box, paint the wood all over with a mixture of one part seaweed plant food diluted with one part water.

5 Fill the box with the sacks of bulbs and the terracotta pots. Plant labels and a small bag of bulb fibre may also be added.

28

DECORATED RUBBER BOOTS

For those gardeners of a more agricultural than horticultural inclination, whose rubber boots are permanently caked in a thick layer of mud, the idea of decorating their boots may seem risible. For the less earnest gardener, this is an attractive way of personalizing and decorating utilitarian footwear. In households with stacks of boots at the back door, it also has the advantage of making your pair immediately apparent. An illustrated flora is a good source of botanical illustrations and, depending on your ability, you can either sketch them straight on to the boot or take a tracing. The design used here is of a dandelion and a daisy with a bee and a butterfly hovering. A design of carrots and tomatoes would be appropriate for a keen vegetable gardener, while roses and ferns would delight a flower arranger. The enamel paints used to paint the design are available in small pots from art shops or DIY centres.

MATERIALS AND EQUIPMENT
rubber boots
soft pencil
felt-tip pen
enamel paints: yellow, green and white
small paintbrush

1 Trace or draw your chosen design on to the boots using a soft pencil.

Below: Alternative designs may be painted on the other boot.

2 When the design is complete, draw over the outline with a felt-tip pen.

3 Paint the main areas of the design and leave to dry overnight.

4 Check that the painted area is fully dry, then paint the details.

5 Leave to dry for at least three days before wearing the boots.

SEED PACKETS

When a favourite plant sets seed, it is a nice gesture to collect some of the seeds and pass them on to friends. The usual way of doing this is to put the seeds into an envelope or plastic bag and to write on the name of the plant. These colourful seed packets are a decidedly more attractive way of passing on the garden's bounty. They require a little forethought, but the results are so stunning that it is definitely worth the effort. Photographs of the flowers are mounted on an outline of the seed packet and then copied on a colour photocopier to produce the required number of packets for each flower. If you don't have access to a colour copier, colour photocopies can be made at print shops and stationers and are relatively inexpensive. Provided you have taken the photographs when the plants were looking their best and have saved the seeds, making the packets can be delayed until the winter months, when you can spend a rainy day making some truly original Christmas presents for other keen gardeners. The back of the packet can be used to write information on how to grow the enclosed seeds and the expected height and spread of the plant.

MATERIALS AND EQUIPMENT
sheets of A4 paper
pencil
15 x 10 cm (6 x 4 in) photographs
glue
cutting mat or thick card
scalpel or scissors
metal ruler
double-sided tape
seeds

1 Draw two seed packets on a sheet of A4 paper, following the template at the back of the book.

2 Photocopy one sheet for each two photographs you will be using. Trim as necessary and mount the photographs on the photocopied pages with glue. Make the required number of colour photocopies of each page.

3 Cut round the packet outline using a scalpel or scissors and metal ruler.

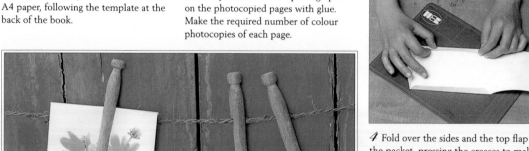

4 Fold over the sides and the top flap of the packet, pressing the creases to make a neat edge.

5 Slip the back of the packet under the side flaps and fasten with double-sided tape or glue. Fill with seeds and fasten the flap with double-sided tape.

LEFT: The front of the packet needs no labelling. On the reverse, write the name of the plant, the date and cultivation instructions.

THE GARDENER'S RETREAT

Inspirational projects for useful and decorative objects to add character to the potting shed and the garden using stencils, decoupage, paint effects and wirework.

While a corner of the garage will be adequate for storing the lawn mower and a few other large garden tools, sooner or later most gardeners aspire to owning a potting shed in which to practise the more esoteric and creative gardening arts. The potting shed is truly the engine of the garden; it is here that the gardener makes and mends, dreams and devises. Depending on the owner's particular temperament, the shed may be anything from utilitarian, well organized and ordered to deeply romantic with chaotic interiors, dim light and dusty nooks and crannies.

The gardener's retreat comes in many shapes and

sizes, from the rather grand brick outbuildings which were an essential part of the Victorian kitchen garden, through the simple wooden structures which can be bought at garden centres, to the idiosyncratic and

TOP: Sunflowers adorn the entrance to the shed.
ABOVE RIGHT AND LEFT: Romantic or utilitarian, the potting shed is the starting point for the gardener's dreams.

characterful edifices which are constructed from "found" materials. The potting shed on the previous page was built out of pieces of reclaimed wood. Builders' skips can be a rich source of well-weathered timber, window frames and doors which can be used to add character to the most ordinary of buildings, or to build from scratch if you are feeling adventurous. Ideally, a potting shed should be tucked into a suitable corner where its contents may spill outdoors without impinging on the garden. Canes and beanpoles are stacked against one wall and a water butt collects rain from the roof. An old table leans against one of the exterior walls to provide an *al fresco* work bench for fine weather; below its weathered surface there is a useful storage area for pots and sacks of compost.

Inside the shed, a long, high bench under the window allows the gardener to work without bending when sowing seeds, pricking out seedlings or taking cuttings. Shelves fill the walls and are stacked with all the clutter of the gardener's realm: packets of seeds, bags of bulbs, tools, fertilizers, pesticides, a few well-thumbed reference books and seed catalogues and the many other

ABOVE RIGHT: Practical concerns often demand a degree of order.
ABOVE: The fruits of the gardener's labours also have their place in the shed.

odds and ends useful to the gardener. Hooks are screwed into the walls and ceiling and hung from these are the larger tools, sieves, shears and reels of wire, all making their contribution to the unique atmosphere of practicality and reverie which presides in the potting shed.

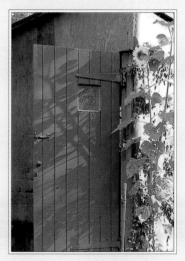

For the gardener's comfort and pleasure, the potting shed should also contain a sturdy but well-worn stool and a battered transistor radio. Cuttings from the garden may be placed casually in a well-used jug or pot. With such a private kingdom, no matter how small, any gardener may find fulfilment and happiness.

TOP: *String, pots and other paraphernalia.*

ABOVE LEFT AND OPPOSITE: *Tools can be stored in a customized storage box or hung on the walls of the shed.*

ABOVE RIGHT: *The entrance to the gardener's retreat.*

DECORATED HAND TOOLS

Trowels and forks are easily mislaid in the border when the telephone rings, a friend arrives or something else distracts the gardener from the matter in hand. They frequently reappear some time later, generally long after they have been replaced by another earth-toned version, equally ambitious to lose itself as soon as possible. Evidently it is not in the interest of the manufacturers to make their tools more visible, as sales would fall dramatically, but a little time spent in the potting shed can transform your next replacement into a distinctive and decorative hand tool. Children's insect stickers are glued on to the brightly coloured handle and then sealed with several layers of varnish to ensure durability. For those of a delicate disposition, whose skin crawls at the thought of insects, flower stickers can be used instead.

3 Glue the stickers on to the handles and leave the glue to dry.

4 Apply several coats of satin-finish varnish, leaving to dry between coats.

ABOVE AND RIGHT: Plain hand tools may get lost in the garden. Bright paint and eye-catching motifs will make them easy to spot in the flowerbed.

MATERIALS AND EQUIPMENT
wooden-handled tools
fine-grade sandpaper
yellow gloss paint
paintbrushes
sheet of stickers
PVA glue
satin-finish varnish

1 Rub down the wooden handles of the tools with fine-grade sandpaper.

2 Paint the handles with two coats of gloss paint, leaving the paint to dry between coats.

VEGETABLE SACKS

Hessian sacks are ideal for storing root vegetables in good condition in the shed, especially when they are hung on hooks so that the air can circulate freely and mice can be kept at bay. Fringed calico squares decorated with stencilled vegetable motifs are stitched on to the sacks to make them decorative as well as functional. Alternatively, if you don't grow vegetables, these sacks can be adapted to make attractive covers for garden cushions.

ABOVE: *Stencilled motifs immediately identify the contents of the sacks.*

MATERIALS AND EQUIPMENT
*tracing paper
pencil
stencil card
aerosol glue
stencil knife
cutting mat or thick card
acrylic or fabric paints
stencil brush
calico, 20 x 25 cm (8 x 10 in), with edges fringed
scrap paper or kitchen roll
hessian, 40 x 120 cm (16 x 48 in)
dressmaker's pins
sewing machine or needle
matching cotton thread*

1 Trace the vegetable stencil templates from the back of the book.

2 Stick the tracing to the stencil card with aerosol glue.

3 Cut out the design with a stencil knife, protecting the work surface with a cutting mat or thick card.

4 Prepare your paints and stencil the design on to the calico using a stippling action. The stencil brush should be as dry as possible for successful stencilling, so have a piece of scrap paper or kitchen roll handy to wipe off excess paint before you begin.

5 Apply more paint in a stippling motion to one side of the carrot, onion and potato for a three-dimensional effect. Leave the paint to dry.

6 Fold the hessian in half, so that it measures 40 x 60 cm (16 x 24 in). Position the stencilled panel on the front of the hessian and pin in place so that it is neatly centred.

7 Stitch the panel in place and then make up the sack. Finish all raw edges with double seam or zig-zag stitch to prevent fraying.

DECOUPAGE SEED STORAGE BOX

Some seeds will still germinate after thousands of years, while others have a far briefer span in which they remain capable of germination. Nowadays, seeds come with a "use by" date printed on the packet and, where indicated, the seeds can be saved for use the next year. Thrown into an empty pot in the corner of the shed, they may just survive attack by damp and insects, but a far better bet is to store them in a tin or box with a snugly fitting lid. An old biscuit tin will do the job, but if you prefer something more decorative, this simple decoupage technique is ideal. Old engravings of fruit and vegetables are photocopied and glued on to a tin-topped wooden box before being sealed with varnish to make an attractive and practical seed storage box in which to keep seeds in optimum condition for next year.

3 Mix up a small amount of wallpaper paste following the manufacturer's instructions. Brush paste on to the reverse side of the images. Position the images evenly over the lid and the sides of the box. As the paste dries slowly, you may reposition as necessary.

Above: Isolated areas of the images can be hand-tinted with watercolour paint.

MATERIALS AND EQUIPMENT
*PVA glue
paintbrushes
photocopies of fruit and vegetable
engravings
scalpel or sharp nail scissors
cutting mat or thick card
wallpaper paste
box or tin, approximately 23 x 23 cm
(9 x 9 in)
water-based matt varnish
artist's raw umber acrylic paint
(optional)*

1 Dilute one part PVA glue with two parts water and brush over the photocopied sheets to "set" the ink and ensure that the paper does not stretch. Leave to dry.

2 Cut round the images with the scalpel, protecting the work surface with a cutting mat or thick card. Alternatively the images can be cut out using a pair of very sharp nail scissors.

4 When the paste is fully dry, seal the lid with several coats of water-based matt varnish, allowing each coat to dry completely before applying the next. To give the box an aged appearance, add a little raw umber acrylic paint to the varnish and mix well. To create an even more antiqued effect, the box may be finished with a crackle glaze (available from good art shops).

PROVENÇAL WATERING CAN

There was a time when it appeared that the old-fashioned metal watering can would be permanently abandoned in favour of the lighter plastic alternative. Plastic cans are sadly lacking in style and cannot be left around the garden as decorative objects in their own right, whereas the classic metal can is both attractive and functional. Not long ago, old watering cans could be bought for next to nothing, but there has been a recent appreciable increase in prices as garden tools become desirable collectables. They are worth buying, however, especially if they are in good condition and

pleasingly shaped. Grouped together in the garden, they become an attractive feature as well as providing an opportunity to involve visitors in the watering. An old can really needs no additional embellishment but a traditionally shaped modern can is ripe for decoration. An engraving of an olive branch was the inspiration for this project. The engraving is photocopied and hand-coloured before being glued on to the painted surface and sealed. In spite of its delicate appearance, the decoration will last for many years as it is protected by several coats of varnish.

MATERIALS AND EQUIPMENT
galvanized metal watering can
turquoise satin-finish oil-based paint
paintbrushes
scalpel
cutting mat or thick card
colouring pencils or crayons
PVA glue
soft cloth
matt varnish

2 Make four photocopies of the olive branch motif at the back of the book. Cut carefully round them with a scalpel, protecting the work surface with a cutting mat or thick card.

3 Colour the photocopies, picking out the leaves in green and highlighting the olives with a strong blue.

4 Seal the coloured motifs with a mixture of one part PVA glue to two parts water. Leave to dry.

1 Paint the watering can with two coats of turquoise satin-finish oil-based paint. Leave to dry fully between coats.

5 Coat the reverse of the motifs with undiluted PVA glue and position on the watering can. Use a soft cloth to wipe off any excess glue. Leave to dry. Protect the watering can with several layers of matt varnish, allowing the varnish to dry fully between coats.

LEFT: Varnish will allow the can to withstand all but the roughest treatment.

PLANT LABELS

Any plant bought at a garden centre will be clearly labelled, but although the printed labels are extremely informative, they are far more functional than attractive. A practical solution is to store the labels in the potting shed for reference if needed and replace them with colourful home-made labels. Unpainted wooden labels can be bought at garden centres or made at home using thin plywood. Coloured varnishes, available in small tins, are used to paint the labels. Buy red, yellow and blue and you can increase the colour range by mixing paints to get orange and green.

MATERIALS AND EQUIPMENT
unpainted wooden labels
fine-grade sandpaper
selection of coloured varnishes
paintbrushes
drill (optional)
garden string (optional)

1 Rub down the labels with fine-grade sandpaper to remove any rough edges.

2 Apply a coat of coloured varnish and leave to dry. Depending on the richness of the colour required, further coats may be added.

3 If required, drill a hole in the pointed end of the label and thread with garden string for hanging.

LEFT: Richly coloured labels can be used to complement the colour of the plant.

ROW MARKERS

In early spring, when the vegetable garden is little more than a patch of bare soil with seeds secretly germinating out of sight, there is a risk of losing track of just what has been planted where. Ordinary labels used as row markers can be kicked over, misplaced when pulled out to read what is written on them or even pulled up by birds. These unusual large-scale row markers are both decorative and functional.

You will be in no doubt as to where you have planted your vegetables and will be able to read what has been planted and when without kneeling down in the damp spring soil. The markers are made from broom handles and wooden knobs bought from a DIY store and are embellished with painted metal labels. They may also be used as decorative label holders for special trees or shrubs.

MATERIALS AND EQUIPMENT
wooden broom handles
ruler
saw
fine-grade sandpaper
wooden knobs, 4 cm (1½ in) in diameter
PVA glue
matt woodwash or emulsion paint
paintbrush
metal plant labels
gold marker pen
garden string
drill (optional)

RIGHT: *Terracotta pots on bamboo canes can also be used as appealing row markers.*

1 For each marker, cut a 70 cm (28 in) length of broom handle. Rub down the cut edge with fine-grade sandpaper and attach a wooden knob using PVA glue. Leave to dry overnight.

2 Paint the row marker with one or two coats of matt woodwash or emulsion paint. Leave to dry.

3 Brush a coat of paint onto the label. Leave to dry, then rub down lightly with fine sandpaper for a distressed look.

4 Carefully outline the label with a gold marker pen. Attach the label to the marker. You can do this either by tying garden string around the knob or by drilling a hole through the marker just below the knob and threading the garden string through.

DECORATIVE PLANT SUPPORT

Broom handles are again the central ingredient of this plant support, which is ideal for growing climbers and shrubs. There are many lovely plant supports on the market, but they are generally expensive to buy and can be quite bulky. This easy-to-assemble alternative is cheap to make,

looks good, and when not in use, it can be folded away until it is needed again. Its finished height is approximately 1.2 m (4 ft), so it is recommended for supporting gentle climbers, such as sweet peas, rather than rampant scramblers. It is not suitable for supporting large shrubs.

MATERIALS AND EQUIPMENT
3 wooden knobs, 4 cm (1½ in) in diameter
3 broom handles
PVA glue
matt woodwash or emulsion paint
paintbrush
drill
sisal rope
tape measure
craft knife

1 Glue a wooden knob on to the end of each broom handle with PVA glue. Leave to dry overnight.

2 Paint all three supports with two coats of matt woodwash or emulsion paint, leaving to dry fully between coats.

3 Drill a hole through each support large enough to take the rope.

4 Cut a 40 cm (16 in) length of sisal rope and thread it through the holes in each support. Tie the rope in a reef knot (that is, left over right and then right over left).

5 Tie a knot approximately 7.5 cm (3 in) from each end of the rope to prevent it unravelling and fray the ends for a decorative effect.

LEFT: A wicker and bamboo structure provides support, and blends unobtrusively into its surroundings.

WIRE HANGING

This decorative hanging is formed from different gauges of garden wire, twigs picked up in the garden and feathers discarded by a bird. When it is hanging from a tree, the slightest breeze sets the feathers in motion and draws the eye. It looks particularly beautiful as it twirls from a branch in a bare winter garden. Making this hanging could be the starting point for creating other decorative objects made from materials found readily to hand. What better way to spend a wet afternoon in the potting shed than making pretty and original gifts like this one?

MATERIALS AND EQUIPMENT
pliers
2 lengths of thick plastic-coated garden wire, 45 cm (18 in)
reel of thin plastic-coated garden wire
pencil
2 twigs, approximately 18 cm (7 in) long
three feathers
black cotton thread

ABOVE: *You can use garden wire for a variety of designs. It is robust enough to withstand all weathers.*

1 Use the pliers to bend the two thick pieces of wire into smooth curly S shapes. Try to match the shapes of the two lengths.

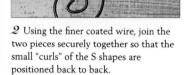

2 Using the finer coated wire, join the two pieces securely together so that the small "curls" of the S shapes are positioned back to back.

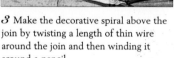

3 Make the decorative spiral above the join by twisting a length of thin wire around the join and then winding it around a pencil.

4 Remove the pencil and trim the wire to 10 cm (4 in) long.

5 Wire the twigs together into a V shape using the fine wire, then fasten them to the top of the base structure.

6 Tie the feathers together using black cotton thread and suspend below the decoration.

7 Tie a length of cotton to the top of the decoration where the two twigs meet and use this to hang the decoration in your chosen position.

GARDENER'S STORAGE BOX

With the best will in the world, it is hard to keep all the little bits and pieces used in the garden under control. Here is a delightful idea for the potting shed which may make the task slightly easier. A small and inexpensive undecorated set of storage drawers is given a decorative coat of varnish and then each drawer is "labelled" by stapling a sample of the contents onto the outside. This ensures that all those small necessary items have a permanent home and you will know exactly where to find them.

MATERIALS AND EQUIPMENT
unpainted set of storage drawers
blue-green wood varnish
paintbrush
coarse-grade sandpaper
sisal string
ruler
scissors
samples of vine-eyes, plant rings, etc.
stapler and staples

1 Paint the front and sides of the boxes and the outer shell with varnish. Leave to dry thoroughly.

2 Rub down with sandpaper to give the box an aged effect, paying particular attention to the corners and edges.

3 Cut a 7.5 cm (3 in) length of string for each drawer.

4 Position the sample item (a plant ring, for example) on the front of the drawer and staple the string to the drawer in two places to hold it in position.

5 As the finishing touch, fray the ends of the string.

BELOW: *A flat wooden tray can also be used to contain clutter.*

GARDENER'S UTILITY RACK

The potting shed tends to attract oddments of materials – this rack not only gives you a chance to store them, but will allow you to use up odd lengths of wire and chicken wire. The shelf at the bottom of the rack is wide enough to hold four food cans. Stripped of their labels, the cans make attractive storage containers that complement the design of the rack. Alternatively, the shelf will hold three small plant pots. Hang the rack in the house, studio, garage or shed. Screwed to the wall at each looped point, it will be quite secure and capable of holding a considerable weight.

MATERIALS AND EQUIPMENT
*straining wire
ruler
wire cutters
permanent marker pen
round-nosed pliers
thin galvanized wire 1.65 mm (0.065
in) and 0.65 mm (0.025 in) thick
general-purpose pliers
tacking wire
gloves
small gauge chicken wire*

1 To make the frame, cut a 2 m (6 ft) length of straining wire. Twist the ends tightly to stop them unravelling and, with a permanent marker pen, mark the wire at intervals of 29.5 cm (11½ in), 5 cm (2 in), 33 cm (13 in), 5 cm (2 in), 25 cm (10 in), 5 cm (2 in), 25 cm (10 in), 5 cm (2 in), 33 cm (13 in), 5 cm (2 in) and 29.5 cm (11½ in). Using round-nosed pliers, make a loop with each 5 cm (2 in) section, making sure that the pen marks match up and that all the loops face outwards.

2 Using the 0.65 mm (0.025 in) galvanized wire, bind the two 29.5 cm (11½ in) sections together to make the bottom of the frame.

3 To make the shelf, cut a 72 cm (29 in) length of straining wire and mark it at intervals of 2.5 cm (1 in), 9 cm (3½ in), 10 cm (4 in), 30 cm (12 in), 10 cm (4 in), 9 cm (3½ in) and 2.5 cm (1 in). Using general-purpose pliers, bend the wire at right angles at these points.

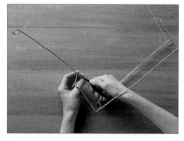

4 Mark each side of the frame 10 cm (4 in) from the bottom. Twist the 2.5 cm (1 in) ends of the shelf wire tightly around the frame at these points.

5 To make the rim and sides of the shelf, cut a 104 cm (41 in) length of 1.65 mm (0.065 in) galvanized wire and mark it at intervals of 2.5 cm (1 in), 13 cm (5 in), 9 cm (3½ in), 13 cm (5 in), 30 cm (12 in), 13 cm (5 in), 9 cm (3½ in), 13 cm (5 in) and 2.5 cm (1 in). Using round-nosed pliers, make a loop with the 2.5 cm (1 in) section at each end of the wire. Bend the wire at the 13 cm (5 in) and 9 cm (3½ in) points at each end at 45° angles to form the side crosses of the shelf. Bend the 30 cm (12 in) section in the middle at right angles to form the top rim.

6 Tack the loops at the ends of the rim wire to the 10cm (4 in) markings on the sides of the main frame. Tack each corner of the side crosses to the frame.

7 Wearing gloves for protection, lay the frame on to the flat piece of chicken wire and cut round the frame. Allow 30 cm (12 in) at the bottom for wrapping around the shelf, so that there is a double thickness of chicken wire at the front of the shelf where it tucks inside. Using 0.65 mm (0.025 in) galvanized wire, bind the edges of the chicken wire to the frame. Wrap any rough edges at the top around the frame before binding. Bind the shelf firmly to the frame as you bind on the chicken wire and remove the tacking wire.

THE FLOWER GARDEN

Stunning decorative ideas for presenting flowers from the garden, from making the most of fragrant roses to symbolic gifts hidden in the meaning of flowers.

Even experienced gardeners who have spent most of their lives growing plants still find it miraculous that a small brown seed sown in the winter-chilled potting shed in March will, by the end of the summer, be a large and flourishing plant covered in flowers. The sunflower, above all, epitomizes this extraordinary and magical transformation. This giant among flowers is the stuff of fairy tales as it shoots skyward to be crowned by its irresistible golden flowers. For a new gardener, it provides maximum results and excitement for minimum effort and can be the stepping stone to growing many other wonderful flowers.

If we think of the different areas of the garden as being like rooms in a house, then surely the flower garden is the outdoor equivalent of the sitting room. This is the area in which we usually choose to entertain our friends, spend time with the family or simply relax in the sunshine, and here our own horticultural preferences are most evident. Just as the sitting room reveals a liking for chintz, Regency stripe or vivid contemporary prints, so the

flower garden reveals our favourite flowers. Gardeners with a love of the informal will often choose a riot of brightly hued cottage-garden flowers, while others prefer the soft tones and sweet scents of a romantic garden filled with roses, lavender and lilies and the modernist gardener may keep flowers to a minimum among interesting textured surfaces and architectural plants.

Of course, the reality is that few of us start our flower garden with a blank canvas, for we inherit

LEFT: *Flowers plucked straight from the garden do not need to be arranged elaborately.*

62

much from the previous gardener. This means that gardening is often more a matter of adaptation than design. This is not necessarily a bad thing; gardens planned and planted by designers are often wonderful to look at and beautifully executed but they are someone else's interpretation of your taste rather than your own. Just as your home gains character from the accumulation of things bought and given to you over many years, so the garden becomes more interesting when each plant has been grown or chosen personally.

Gardeners are notoriously critical of their own gardens: "You should have seen the garden last week" is a common cry. However, if your flower garden fulfils the following criteria, you should be happy that you have achieved what most gardeners aspire to: it contains something of interest most of the year; it provides some cut flowers and cuttings, seeds or small plants to give away to friends; its maintenance is usually more enjoyable than stressful or exhausting; and, most important of all, it gives you pleasure and satisfaction.

There is a danger that devising projects for the flower garden may result in "gilding the lily", so most of the projects in this chapter are ideas for presenting and displaying plants rather than an attempt to compete with the matchless beauty of the flowers themselves.

ABOVE RIGHT: A few interesting containers and hanging baskets may be all you need to provide interest in the flower garden.
LEFT: The natural beauty of beds and borders speaks for itself.

THE FRAGRANT ROSE

The rose has been loved and cultivated for many thousands of years. It has two strands of origin, one in China and the other in Europe and the Middle East. The modern rose we know today is the result of the interbreeding of these ancestors. Historically, the rose was valued not only for its beauty, but also for its incomparable fragrance, and today rose oil remains an important ingredient of fine perfumes. Apart from their commercial value, roses have long been grown as garden flowers and it is still possible to buy varieties of roses today which were first recorded hundreds of years ago. Unfortunately, many of these older varieties flower only for a brief time and are prone to disease.

There was a time, not long ago, when commercial rose breeders put most of their energy into producing plants which overcame these problems, but in the process much of the perfume was lost. Fortunately, there has been something of a reversal in this trend and breeders are now producing long-flowering roses with many of the characteristics of the old varieties, including their glorious fragrance.

ABOVE: The simplest arrangement of roses from the garden captures the essence of summer.

A scented rose is a welcome addition to most gardens, and even the smallest terrace can accommodate a rose in a pot. Where space is a consideration, the modern "English" roses are ideal, as they embody the qualities of the old roses with the virtues of the newer varieties. But to enjoy the fragrance of the rose at its headiest, four roses in particular have been judged to have the finest scent of all. They are "Belle de Crécy", a pink-flowered Gallica rose; "Louise Odier", a long-flowering Bourbon with strong pink flowers; "Madame Isaac Pereire", a large Bourbon with pink flowers which can also be grown as a climber; and "Roseraie de l'Hay" with its carmine pink flowers on a large, very thorny bush. Of these, "Louise Odier" is the most compact and suitable for an average-sized garden, while the others are best in a large border.

LEFT: A scented rose bush makes a lovely gift, and could be accompanied by handwritten recipes for making rose-petal jam and pot-pourri.

ROSE POT-POURRI

The fragrance of roses can be captured by drying the petals for pot-pourri. For the most intense scent, pick the roses early in the day, after any dew has dried. Spread the petals on a rack and leave to dry in a warm place. Store in sealed containers away from the light until you are ready to make the pot-pourri. A well-made pot-pourri will remain fragrant for many months, and makes a lovely gift when made with flowers from your own garden.

INGREDIENTS AND EQUIPMENT
1 tbsp/15 ml ground cinnamon
1 tbsp/15 ml powdered orris root
1 whole nutmeg, grated
mortar and pestle
40 drops rose geranium oil
30 drops rose oil
20 drops lavender oil
10 drops bergamot oil
1.75 litres/3 pints/7½ cups rose petals,
rosebuds and rose leaves (peony flowers
and petals and lavender flowers may
also be included)
large bowl
spoon
lidded ceramic or glass container

1 Mix together the cinnamon, orris root and nutmeg in a mortar.

2 Add the essential oils and blend to a moist powder using the pestle.

3 Measure the flower petals into a large bowl and thoroughly mix in the oil and spice mixture.

WARNING
Certain essential oils should not be handled by anyone who is or may be pregnant or where there is an existing medical condition. If in any doubt consult your doctor. Some oils can irritate sensitive skin and it is therefore advisable to wear rubber gloves when handling the concentrated oil and spice blends.

4 Put the mixture in a large, lidded ceramic or glass container and leave to cure (the process in which the different aromas blend into a homogeneous fragrance) for six weeks, stirring occasionally. The pot-pourri is now ready for use.

ROSE-PETAL JAM

Those fortunate enough to have large numbers of roses in their garden may also like to try their hand at making rose-petal jam. This was popular in Tudor England and, although seldom seen nowadays, it remains a popular conserve in the Middle East. It is best made with strongly scented, deep-red damask roses, which must be free of chemical sprays. As with the pot-pourri, the roses should be picked early in the day. The flowers should be open, but not full-blown. The contents of the pan as you stew the rose petals will look decidedly unattractive but will smell wonderful. The addition of the sugar will restore the rich colour of the roses. If boiled too long, this jam will crystallize because of the high proportion of sugar, but this will not detract from the flavour and the fragrance. If necessary, the jam can be melted by placing the jar in a pan of warm water. Pack in attractive jars with a presentation label.

INGREDIENTS AND EQUIPMENT
rose flowers
scissors
lidded pan
sugar (3 times the weight of the rose
petal mixture)
spoon
sterilized jars

1 Remove the petals from the flower heads and snip off the white bases. Discard any that are discoloured or spoiled.

2 Place the petals in a lidded pan and pour in enough water to cover.

3 Stew the petals until tender; this can take 10–30 minutes.

4 Weigh the mixture, then multiply by three and weigh out this amount of sugar. Gradually add the sugar, stirring until it has all dissolved.

5 Bring to a rapid boil and test for setting point.

6 Decant into warm, sterilized jars and seal. Label the jars when cool.

PAINTED TRUG

The traditional trug is a piece of garden equipment which has endured and is still much appreciated for its practicality, durability and fine design. Solid wooden trugs have been used for many centuries, but the design with which we are familiar, inspired by the coracle boat, was invented by Thomas Smith in 1820. The company he founded is still making trugs today. The handles and rim are traditionally made from coppiced sweet chestnut, while the seven boards which form the basket shape are made from cricket-bat willow. A "modern" version, dating back a mere 60 years, is made from birch ply. Properly looked after, a trug can be expected to last between 40 and 50 years so, although relatively expensive to buy, they are a life-time investment. Given the history and materials of the trug, it may seem disrespectful to attempt any embellishments to what is clearly already a superior product, but with all those decades of use stretching ahead, the occasional change of colour scheme seems permissible, especially when using woodstains which will help to protect the wood.

ABOVE: *A similar trug treated with a mauve woodstain.*

MATERIALS AND EQUIPMENT
trug
scrubbing brush
woodstains: yellow and blue
paintbrush
medium-grade sandpaper

1 Scrub the trug if necessary. Mix green woodstain by combining some of the blue and yellow.

2 Paint the outside body of the trug blue and the inside green.

3 Paint the rim and handle of the trug yellow. Leave to dry.

4 Rub over the trug with sandpaper to give it a mellow appearance.

SHAKESPEARE'S FLOWERS

Those of a literary bent can put together a collection of some of the flowers mentioned in Shakespeare. His writings are peppered with references to both wild and cultivated flowers. A wooden basket holds the plants, which are wrapped in hessian and tied with string to give the gift a suitably Shakespearean appearance. The plants used here are rue, lavender, rosemary and thyme, but there are many others to choose from, including gillyflower (wallflower), columbine, daffodil, daisy, flower-de-luce (iris florentina), heart's ease (pansy), honeysuckle, lily, marigold, marjoram and violet. For the real enthusiast, these first few plants could be the starting point for a Shakespearean garden.

MATERIALS AND EQUIPMENT
*4 pieces of hessian, 40 x 40 cm
(16 x 16 in)
4 Shakespearean plants as listed above
garden string
scissors
basket
gift tag*

1 Remove some of the threads from the edges of the hessian squares to make a fringed border.

2 Wrap each plant in a piece of hessian, ensuring that the plant pot is concealed. Tie with string. Arrange the plants in the basket. Attach a gift tag to the handle.

LEFT: *Write the recipient's name on the tag, with a relevant quotation on the back.*

BOX OF BUTTERFLIES

Butterflies flitting from plant to plant are among the flower garden's most engaging sights. To encourage them to visit your garden, plant the flowers which attract them and, if possible, leave a corner of the garden for nettles to grow undisturbed, as this is the food plant of the caterpillars of many of the beautiful fritillary butterflies, including the red admiral, peacock and tortoiseshell butterflies. Nectar-producing flowers favoured by butterflies include aubrietia, wallflowers and polyanthus in spring; honesty, valerian, sweet rocket, petunias, lavender, marjoram, hyssop and buddleia in summer; and sedum and Michaelmas daisies in autumn. For this project, a rather tatty old box, bought very cheaply in a junk shop, has been given a new string covering to its handle and decorated with a stencil of butterflies. If you are unable to obtain a suitable old container, you can "age" a new one by diluting the ink used for the stencils with water and painting the box with the mixture. You can make your own wire handle from thick garden wire. Drill a hole centrally in each side of the box, thread the wire through and form into a curved handle. Trim the ends protruding from the box and bend them back on themselves to fix the handle in position. Three "butterfly" plants, lavender, marjoram and sedum, are packed into the box and surrounded with bark as a finishing touch.

MATERIALS AND EQUIPMENT
tracing paper
pencil
stencil card
aerosol glue
stencil knife or scalpel
cutting mat or thick card
brown acrylic ink or paint
plate
wooden box with handle
stencil brush
sisal string
scissors
"butterfly" plants as listed above
ornamental bark

1 Trace the butterfly template from the back of the book on to tracing paper.

2 Mount the tracing on a piece of stencil card using the aerosol glue.

3 Cut out the stencil with a stencil knife or scalpel, protecting the work surface with a cutting mat or thick card.

4 Pour some of the ink or paint thinned with water on to a plate.

5 Stencil the design on to the sides and ends of the box in a random pattern. You can use the other side of the stencil, provided it is dry, to make the butterflies fly in different directions.

LEFT: Stylized stencilled butterflies embellish the gift box.

RIGHT: The plants will bring butterflies to the garden.

6 Wrap sisal string around the wire handle. Tie firmly at each end to ensure that it does not unravel.

7 Place the plants in the box and use the bark to cover the tops of the pots and fill the spaces in between.

TRIBUTE TO MONET

Anyone fortunate enough to have visited Monet's beautiful house and garden will appreciate the vivid colours to be seen in both. One of his favourite colour combinations was blue and yellow, and this project uses both these colours to decorate a simple wire basket. The basket is then lined with moss and planted with richly coloured pansies in a tribute to the great artist's glorious palette and his passionate love of gardening and gardens.

MATERIALS AND EQUIPMENT
wooden-handled wire basket
masking tape
blue car-spray paint
large cardboard box
yellow woodstain
paintbrush
moss
3 pansies
compost

1 Mask the handle of the basket with masking tape and spray the basket blue. It is better to apply two or three thin coats than one thick one, as the paint has a tendency to run if applied too thickly. Leave to dry between applications. Use the spray paint in a well-ventilated area and place the basket in a large cardboard box lying on its side to limit the spread of the fine droplets of paint. Avoid inhaling the fumes. Leave to dry completely.

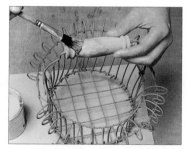

2 Remove the masking tape from the handle and paint it with the yellow woodstain. Leave to dry, then add further coats for a more intense colour. Leave to dry completely.

3 Line the basket with moss and, removing the pansies from their pots, plant them in the basket. Fill around the plants with extra compost if necessary and then tuck more moss around them. Water well and leave to drain.

LEFT: Rich red pansies complement the blue and yellow of the basket.

SEASONAL GIFT BOXES AND BASKETS

In the gardening world, plants are always in circulation as gardeners pass on seedlings or cuttings from favourite plants. This generosity is much appreciated and reciprocated and it is undoubtedly the best way for the rich tapestry of a flower garden to develop. There can be a delightful uncertainty about the process of exchanging plants, the names of which are sometimes forgotten or never known. These plants are often referred to by the name of the person who gave them, and neighbours can be somewhat alarmed to overhear an intention to "sort out Mrs Bottomley", who is "running rampant all over the garden". As generous as gardeners are with their plants, they do tend to hand them over without taking much time or trouble over the presentation. This is quite acceptable and appropriate on most occasions, but for those times when you would like to make something more of the plants you are giving, this project suggests some interesting plants to give as presents and ways of making them look even more beautiful. The ideas given here are intended to be inspirational rather than recipes to be followed to the letter.

SUMMER GIFT BASKET

The plants in this basket have been chosen to create a subtle blend of summer scents and colours; they would look wonderful planted in a tub or grouped together in a border. A scented-leaf pelargonium and two other types with richly coloured flowers are packed into the basket with an unusual tender salvia and one white- and one blue-flowered lavender. The plants nestle in straw, which disguises the pots and holds them in position. A gift tag is tied to the basket with a matching deep pink ribbon.

There are endless combinations of plants that can be grouped together as a summer gift and a colour theme is a good starting point. Bear in mind that the collection of plants should enjoy the same growing conditions and grow to a similar height. After all, the marigold and sunflower are both yellow and are a similar height when ready for planting out! The plants used here are: *Pelargonium fragrans variegatum, P.* 'Sancho Panza', an unnamed cerise-flowered zonal *pelargonium, Salvia buchananii, S. greggii* x *lycioides, Lavandula* 'Hidcote' and *L.* 'Alba'.

SPRING GIFT BASKET

Climbing plants are a good choice for a springtime present. Climbers are often more interesting if they are planted alongside one another so that they can intermingle; in some cases, this also lengthens the flowering season. The plants chosen here are two clematis, one a single carmine pink and the other a double white. They are placed in a twig and wire basket which echoes the diamond shape of the protective netting around the flowers. Nothing else is needed to make the gift complete except the addition of a gift tag.

Other plants to consider include scented climbers such as jasmine, honeysuckle and wisteria, while long-flowering climbers such as solanum and passionflower will produce flowers right through the summer to the first frosts. Someone with a large area of wall to cover would be grateful to receive a collection of foliage climbers, including ornamental vines, Virginia creeper and ivies.

AUTUMN GIFT BOX

Shrubs are the ideal plants to give in the autumn as this is the best time to plant them. As autumn tends to be the time of year when the colour range in the garden is limited to reds, yellows and golds, this selection of plants has been chosen to broaden the gardener's palette. A sturdy wooden crate makes an attractive and practical container and allows the plants to be transported with minimum damage. Soft blue-flowered agastache, perovskia and caryopteris and the deep-purple-leaved *Physocarpus* 'Diabolo' and cotinus were used here. When choosing a selection of shrubs, bear in mind the conditions each plant likes best.

ABOVE LEFT AND OPPOSITE: The summer gift basket combines the scents and colours of the season.

PLANT THEATRE

The idea of displaying plants in this way comes from the tradition of Auricula Theatres, which were built in the past to exhibit these much-prized plants. The "theatres" were solid wooden structures, usually built into the corner of a walled garden and painted black to throw the auricula flowers into striking relief. They were lit by lanterns at night to allow the proud owners to display the plants to dinner guests. As auriculas only flower for a fairly brief period in late spring, any structure devoted to this one purpose would be of little use in the modern garden, and as few people have unused corners of a walled garden, this rather grand concept is reduced here to a theatre more relevant to the scale on which most of us now garden. This modest structure is made from scrap timber bought very cheaply from a timber mill, but it could also be made from rough timber bought at a DIY store. The sides and roof are left unfilled to allow as much light as possible to reach the plants and to make watering easy. Placed on a wall opposite a door or window, the theatre can be used to display plants throughout the year, starting with snowdrops or aconites in late winter. With the addition of strings of nuts and other treats, it could also attract birds during cold months. As the spring and summer progress, use the theatre to show off flowers when they are at their peak of perfection. The plants do not need to be exotic or rare.

MATERIALS AND EQUIPMENT
7.5 m (8 yd) of 2.5 x 2.5 cm
(1 x 1 in) rough timber, cut into
the following lengths:
60 cm (24 in) (x 4); 28 cm (11 in)
(x 10); 25 cm (10 in) (x 2); 17 cm
(6½ in) (x 7); 12 cm (4¾ in) (x 4)
PVA glue
glue brush
hammer
nails
woodstain
paintbrush

1 Assemble the base using two 28 cm (11 in) pieces for the bottom shelf and two 12 cm (4¾ in) for the crosspieces. The angle at each corner should be 2.5 x 2.5 cm (1 x 1 in). All the joins are glued as well as nailed for extra rigidity.

2 Assemble the two sides using two 60 cm (24 in), one 17 cm (6½ in) and one 12 cm (4¾ in) pieces for each side. Join the two long pieces together at the centre, using the 12 cm (4¾ in) piece as a crosspiece. Attach the 17 cm (6½ in) piece 2.5 cm (1 in) from one end, with each end of the timber overlapping the parallel side pieces by 2.5 cm (1 in).

3 Attach the open end of the sides to the base as shown in the photo.

4 Add the middle and top shelves using two 28 cm (11 in) pieces for each shelf.

5 To make the apex of the roof, join the two 25 cm (10 in) pieces at right angles to a 28 cm (11 in) piece.

6 Join the two pieces at the apex with a 17 cm (6½ in) crosspiece. Then add further 17 cm (6½ in) crosspieces centrally and at the base.

7 Attach the roof to the shelves.

8 It is a good idea to attach a further piece of 28 cm (11 in) timber across the front of the bottom and middle shelves to keep the pots securely in position (see finished picture).

9 Paint the whole structure with a coat of woodstain.

Above: Traditionally, plant theatres were painted black, and were created to show auriculas to best effect.

THE LANGUAGE OF FLOWERS

There has been a long tradition of attaching meaning to certain flowers which reached its peak when the Victorian leisured classes devised their rather whimsical and arbitrary "language of flowers". In those days, any man wishing to impress a woman who was versed in this language would have to negotiate his way through a minefield of potential dangers, for in some cases it was not simply the variety of flower but also its colour that carried a message. A red carnation signified "alas, my poor heart", while a yellow carnation indicated "disdain" and a striped flower "refusal". Should you receive a posy containing basil ("hatred"), tansy ("I declare war against you"), rue ("disdain"), lavender ("distrust") and double dahlias ("instability"), it would be a fair indication either that the swain had not done his homework or that you had just received the floral equivalent of hate mail. Nowadays, there are fewer pitfalls; roses are universally accepted as a token of love and any bouquet of flowers that does not appear to have been hurriedly grabbed from a garage forecourt is generally a welcome gift. A posy of flowers picked from the garden is always special, and while the selection of flowers should usually be made on the basis of colour and compatibility, it can be fun to consult the Victorian oracle and devise a posy with a message. The posy of sunflowers, fennel, fuchsia, dahlia, sage and fern assembled here carries the message, "I sincerely adore and esteem your praiseworthy good taste"! It is not exactly romantic, but is fun to give to someone who has just done some redecorating or has moved house. To develop the language further, you would need to obtain one of the facsimile editions of the original books.

MATERIALS AND EQUIPMENT
sunflowers ("adoration")
fennel ("worthy of praise")
fuchsia ("taste")
single dahlia ("good taste")
sage ("esteem")
fern ("sincerity")
bucket
garden string
50 cm (20 in) ribbon

1 Remove any foliage at the base of the flower stems. Condition the flowers by standing them in deep water in a bucket in a cool place for a couple of hours.

2 Lay out the flowers on a work surface, grouping them by variety.

RIGHT: Scented pelargonium is a symbol of friendship.

3 Assemble the posy by selecting the flowers a few at a time and, holding the posy loosely in one hand, rearranging until you are happy with the shape.

4 Tie the stems firmly with string to keep your chosen arrangement in shape and decorate with ribbon tied in a pretty bow.

THE HERB GARDEN

Unusual and original ideas for growing culinary and healing herbs with techniques for planting, harvesting and storing.

W ith the advent of pot-grown herbs available at the supermarket throughout the year, it may seem that growing your own plants is no longer as important as it was in the past. Why struggle to germinate basil during a cold spring when it is readily available at the local shop? The answer of course is that, as with so many other aspects of gardening, there is a plea-sure in the process and a greater appreciation of the plant and its qualities when you have followed its progress to maturity.

Herbs have always been vital to our health and well-being and, in the past, they were added to food as much for their medicinal properties as for the savour and flavour they added to the dish. Much of the history of the west-ern world can be charted by the spread of herbs from one centre of

civilization to another. The Saracens brought herbs from the Middle East and physic gardens were culti-vated in monasteries, introducing plants such as rosemary and sage to northern Europe. Their aromatic qualities were as much appreciated as their healing powers by the medieval householder: the unpleasant smells of everyday life were masked by covering the

TOP AND LEFT: Potted herbs are beautiful additions to the garden, and make delightful gifts for less horticulturally inclined friends.

floor with strewing herbs, which also helped to keep bugs at bay; and soothing lotions and potions were produced in great quantities in the still room. Fortunately, many of the old uses for herbs have become redundant and in recent times we have, to a large extent, handed over responsibility for the healing qualities of herbs to the experts, although country remedies, teas and tisanes remain popular.

Although most herbs are not difficult to grow, they will do best if they are given the conditions of their natural habitat. Thyme, rosemary, sage, marjoram and origanum grow wild on the barren hills of Provence, so they will be happiest in a sunny spot in free-draining soil or planted in gritty compost in a large pot. Mint, parsley, chervil and lemon balm thrive in partial shade, while coriander and basil enjoy full sunshine in a moist, but not soggy, soil. Most difficulties occur when trying to grow herbs with different requirements in the same location.

A herb garden can be anything from a pot planted with a few favourite herbs to a formal garden. Whatever its scale, the herb garden's plants will be among the most used and valued in the garden. Plant your herb garden or place your pots near the kitchen door for convenience and position them so that you can brush against them to release their fragrance – that momentary pause to appreciate the scent is a simple gift in a busy life.

Top: A herbal basket containing sage, camomile and golden marjoram as well as wild strawberries and ivy.

Right: Southernwood grows in well-drained soil in a sunny position.

MEDITERRANEAN HERBS

Empty cans are popular plant containers on the Greek islands of the Mediterranean. Painted in brilliant colours and planted with basil, other herbs and geraniums, they stand under the windows and around the doors of the whitewashed houses. Even in cooler climates, the illusion of Mediterranean sunshine and the memory of sun-soaked holidays can be effectively evoked by grouping these brightly coloured cans of herbs against an appropriately coloured background. Ask your local pizza restaurant for some of their empty catering-size cans; they get through huge quantities and shouldn't mind passing them on. Health and safety regulations ensure that the cans have been opened in such a way that there are no sharp edges, but if you obtain your tins from another source, the best way to make the edges safe is to mask them with insulating tape. Smaller cans may be treated in the same way and used as containers for herbs on the kitchen window sill. In this case, don't punch holes in the base of the can. Simply place a small amount of gravel in the bottom for drainage and slip the herb, still in its plastic pot, into the can.

MATERIALS AND EQUIPMENT
empty cans
hammer
nail
insulating tape (optional)
gloss paint
paintbrush
gravel
herbs
compost
coarse grit

1 Turn each can upside down and use the hammer and nail to pierce a series of drainage holes in the base.

2 If the edges of the can are sharp, mask them with insulating tape by wrapping the tape around the outside edge of the tin and folding it over onto the inside.

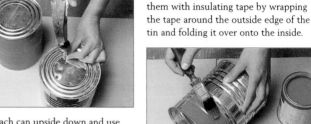

3 Paint the can with one or two layers of gloss paint, depending on how well the paint adheres. Leave to dry fully before planting.

4 Fill the bottom of the can with gravel or a similar drainage material and plant the herb in a mixture of two parts compost to one part coarse grit.

LEFT: These eye-catching containers could not be easier to make. Strong primary colours set off the lush foliage perfectly.

APOTHECARY'S GARDEN

The use of herbal remedies is enjoying renewed popularity as we come to appreciate that, although our forebears may not have understood the biochemical reason for the effectiveness of each remedy, they had a real knowledge of the healing power of herbs. While all medication, natural or otherwise, should be administered with caution and, in cases of an existing illness, only with the consent of a doctor, simple herbal cures and infusions can promote health and well-being and soothe away stress and tension. For this project, herbs are planted in terracotta pots embellished with their botanical names and grouped together in a large, clay saucer as a tribute to the apothecaries of old. This herb garden would make an interesting gift, especially if a herbal guide were included for reference.

3 Fill the saucer with clay granules or gravel and arrange the pots.

Left: Thyme tisane is a purifying drink and an aid to digestion.

MATERIALS
permanent marker pen
5 10 cm (4 in) terracotta pots
selection of herbs:
pot marigold (Calendula): healing and mildly antiseptic
thyme (Thymus): drunk as a tisane, purifying and disinfectant
feverfew (Matricaria): a leaf rolled into a ball of bread can be taken for migraine
lavender (Lavandula): the essential oil is an effective treatment for minor burns and scalds
rosemary (Rosmarinus): use in an infusion as a treatment for scalp problems and an excellent hair rinse
compost (optional)
clay saucer, 36 cm (14 in) in diameter
clay granules or gravel

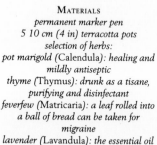

1 Using the marker pen, write the botanical names of the plants around the rims of the pots.

2 Plant the herbs in the pots, using additional compost if necessary.

Right: Rosemary can be used in an infusion for an effective hair rinse.

TOPIARY HERBS

This is one of the most attractive and stylish ways of growing herbs, especially when they are planted in "long tom" pots, which complete the sculptural effect. The herbs suitable for this treatment are those with woody stems such as rosemary, lemon verbena, santolina and lavender. Select young plants with a strong, straight central stem, which can be trimmed to create the topiary shape. Once established, provided the herbs are regularly fed and watered and moved into larger pots as they grow, they should reach a good size and live for a number of years. Bear in mind that the shape of the "long tom" pots makes them dry out more quickly than more conventional pots, so frequent watering is essential. Topiary herbs are attractive as centrepieces for a paved herb garden and individually they make elegant gifts. To display a group of pots to greatest effect, stand them against a plain background so that their shapes will be clearly outlined. Prune to shape every two weeks during the growing season. No special equipment is needed; a pair of scissors will be perfectly adequate. In colder areas, the plants will benefit from some winter protection. Pack them, pots and all, into a large wooden box filled with bark and stand them on a well lit shelf in the potting shed during the winter months and they should survive all but the most extreme cold.

MATERIALS AND EQUIPMENT
scissors
young herb plants: rosemary, lavender,
santolina or lemon verbena
selection of terracotta pots, ideally
"long toms"
compost
coarse grit
washed gravel

1 Use the scissors to trim any side shoots away from the central stem of each plant and to remove the foliage from the bottom half to two-thirds of the stem.

ABOVE: The dramatic shape of the topiary is seen to best advantage against a plain background.

LEFT: Aromatic lavender is popular both for its beauty and culinary uses.

2 Trim the remaining foliage to shape.

3 Transplant the herb into a terracotta pot using a mixture of two parts compost to one part coarse grit. Plant firmly, first gently loosening the herb's root ball to ensure that the roots quickly settle into the new compost.

4 Cover the top layer of compost with a layer of washed gravel. Water well and stand in a sheltered, sunny position.

BLOOMING BORAGE

There is an old country saying that "a garden without borage is a garden without courage", which refers to the old herbalists' belief that this plant has the ability to lift the spirits and gladden the heart. Recently, borage has become an important crop as its oils have been found to be as potent as those of evening primrose, and fields of its stunning blue flowers are a more common sight in the countryside. In addition to their medicinal properties, borage flowers floating in a glass of summer punch have the ability to gladden most hearts. Enthusiasts of summer drinks would be delighted by the gift of a flower-decorated bucket complete with a borage plant.

4 Stencil the outline of the flowers on to the bucket in a random pattern, overlapping them if you like.

5 Use the paintbrush to add details to the flowers in deep blue and white.

6 Place the borage plant in the bucket.

MATERIALS AND EQUIPMENT
tracing paper
pencil
stencil card
aerosol glue
cutting mat or thick card
stencil knife or scalpel
acrylic paints: mid-blue, deep blue and white
plate
stencil brush
galvanized bucket, 18 cm (7 in) in diameter
paintbrush
borage plant

1 Trace the borage flower template from the back of the book on to tracing paper.

2 Mount the tracing on a piece of stencil card using the aerosol glue.

3 Place the stencil card on the cutting mat or thick card and cut out the stencil with a stencil knife or scalpel. Pour some mid-blue paint on to a plate.

RIGHT: *The beautiful blue flowers of the borage plant can be used as a salad garnish or to decorate glasses of refreshing summer punch.*

BOUQUET GARNI

There is a world of difference between fresh or home-dried bouquet garni and the little sachets which sit at the back of most herb racks, slowly losing all resemblance to the fresh herbs from which they were made. The classic bouquet garni consists of parsley, thyme and a bay leaf tied into a posy with string and used to impart flavour to stews, soups and sauces. In Provence, rosemary is always added as well. In all but the coldest areas, it is possible to gather these herbs fresh for the majority of the year, but a small stock of dried bouquet garni, each encased in a little muslin bag, is a good insurance policy against the bleak mid-winter (see the Chef's Herbs project in this chapter for the correct way to dry herbs). To avoid home-made "ancient relics", remember to throw out any remaining dried herbs when you gather the first fresh herbs of the year. For this project, the herbs are planted in a small, moss-lined wooden crate to make a convenient bouquet garni garden for the ledge outside the kitchen window.

MATERIALS AND EQUIPMENT
drill
wooden crate, approximately 25 x 20 x 15 cm (10 x 8 x 6 in)
40 cm (16 in) sisal rope
permanent marker pen
liquid seaweed plant food
paintbrush
moss
small bay tree
thyme
2 parsley plants
compost
coarse grit

1 To make the handles, drill two holes in each end of the wooden crate. Thread a 20 cm (8 in) length of sisal rope through the holes at each end from the outside and knot the ends to secure.

2 Use the permanent marker pen to write on each side of the crate.

3 To give the crate a weathered appearance, paint it with a mixture of one part seaweed plant food and one part water. You can make the mixture more or less dilute depending on the finish required.

4 Line the crate with moss.

5 Plant the herbs, using a mixture of three parts compost to one part coarse grit. Press in the plants firmly and tuck more moss around. Water thoroughly.

LEFT: A fresh bouquet garni – bay, thyme and parsley bound with twine.

SOME LIKE IT HOT

There was a time when chillies were only met with extreme caution and suspicion. Now that the cooking of India, Thailand and Mexico is becoming as familiar as our own, we are all growing acquainted with the expanding range of shapes, sizes and strengths of chillies that are appearing on our supermarket shelves. If you have successfully grown pepper plants in your garden or greenhouse, there is no reason why you shouldn't have a go at growing your own chillies, although they will be milder than those grown in sub-tropical climates. To concentrate the fiery flavour, chillies need very high temperatures while the fruit is developing, so a pot-grown specimen is probably your best bet if you favour the intensely hot taste. Keep the pot in a sunny posi-

tion on the kitchen windowsill until the fruit are well formed and beginning to ripen, then you can move the plant outdoors in full sun to complete the process. Until the chillies begin to ripen, the plant isn't very colourful, but you can brighten it up by painting the pot with a chilli design. Harvest your chillies at different stages of ripeness to experience the varying degrees of strength and sweetness, and dry those you are not going to use immediately by threading their stems on to skewers and hanging them up in a warm place. Once they are fully dried, they can be threaded on to string and hung where they can decorate the kitchen until ready for use. If you wish to preserve their flavour at its best, store in dark glass jars.

PAINTED CHILLI POT

MATERIALS AND EQUIPMENT
terracotta pot, 18 cm (7 in) in diameter
soft pencil
acrylic paints
paintbrush
chilli plant
compost

1 Sketch the chilli design on the pot using a soft pencil.

2 Paint the design using the acrylic paints, mixing the colours to achieve subtler shades. Leave to dry completely.

3 Plant the chilli plant in the pot, water well and stand in a warm position until the fruit are well formed.

DRYING CHILLIES

MATERIALS AND EQUIPMENT
*selection of chillies at varying stages of
ripeness
wooden skewers
2 30 cm (12 in) lengths of chain
string
dark glass jars (optional)*

1 Thread the stems of the chillies onto
the skewers. Prepare four skewers in this
way. Do not overfill the skewers.

2 Thread the skewers onto the chains,
making sure they are sufficiently spaced
to allow air to circulate, and tie in place
with string.

3 Hang in a warm place until the
chillies are dry to the touch, remove
from the skewers and thread on to string
or store in dark glass jars.

CHEF'S HERBS

An old saucepan is a witty and appropriate container for a collection of culinary herbs. The plants remain in their individual pots and stand on a layer of gravel to ensure they remain moist but not waterlogged. As the herbs pass their peak, they can be replaced by new ones to provide the cook with a continuous supply. To get the best from herbs, they should be picked regularly during the growing season and, in most cases, their flavour is at its best before the plant flowers. When herbs are not needed for immediate use, they can be dried and stored. While bunches of herbs hanging from the kitchen ceiling look extremely decorative, this is not the best way to preserve their colour and flavour; they should be dried and stored away from the light.

MATERIALS AND EQUIPMENT
freshly picked herbs
brown paper
scissors
string
airtight glass jars
labels
pen

1 Cut the herbs on a dry day before midday and after any early dew has evaporated.

2 Cut squares of brown paper and place a small bundle of herbs diagonally in the centre of each square.

3 Roll the paper into a cone and secure with string.

4 Hang the cones upside down to dry in a warm, airy place.

5 When the herbs are dry to the touch, remove them from the paper and strip the leaves from the stems.

6 Pack into airtight glass jars and label with the name and harvest date. Store in a cupboard away from the light.

LAVENDER BOTTLES

There was a time when nearly every garden grew lavender bushes and housewives considered harvesting the lavender an essential part of the domestic ritual. Lavender was used in healing and soothing lotions, in flower waters, as a strewing herb and to scent linen. The tradition of scenting linen with lavender originated not in the desire to impart its fragrance to the bedchamber but rather in its considerable insect-repellent properties. The making of lavender bags, sachets and bottles was an essential household task rather than the aromatic pleasure it is today. Much of the lavender that is grown today is the compact form with short flower stems. This is ideal for making bags and sachets where only the flower heads are needed, but if you also grow the taller varieties, you can use them to make lavender bottles. This traditional way of preserving lavender is practical as well as decorative as the stems form a cage around the flower heads, releasing the fragrance but preventing the flowers from dropping. However, a vigorous shake will dislodge some of the flowers and, if you have wooden floors in your home, you can crush a few of the fallen flowers underfoot to fill the room with the scent of lavender. When Victorian ladies made lavender bottles, they wove satin ribbon in and out of the stems and trimmed them with elaborate bows; this was probably a symptom of too much time and too little to do, and this plainer version is less time-consuming to make and more pleasing to modern tastes.

MATERIALS AND EQUIPMENT
FOR EACH LAVENDER BOTTLE:
20 fresh lavender stems
string
scissors or secateurs

2 Holding the flower heads in one hand, use the other hand to fold the stems over the flower heads, one at a time. Work systematically until all the stems are folded over the flower heads and the bottle shape is formed.

3 Tie the stems in place about half-way down their length.

4 Trim the ends of the stems level with scissors or secateurs.

1 Gather the lavender stems into a neat bundle and tie firmly, but not too tightly, with string just beneath the flower heads. Cut off the loose ends of string.

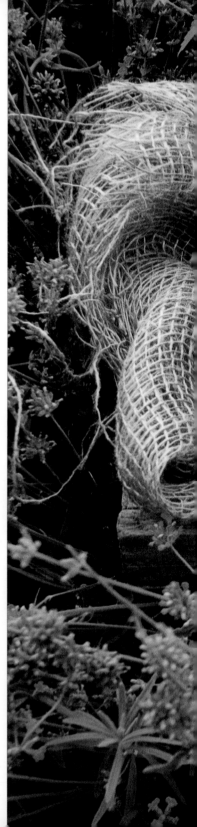

FRESH HERB POSY

There is a long-established tradition of taking a bunch of flowers as a gift when visiting friends, but a posy of home-grown herbs is a more unusual, and very attractive, alternative. The herbs should be picked early in the day and stood in deep water in a cool place to condition them before making the posy. This will ensure that they still look fresh and appetizing when they arrive at their destination. This posy makes a decorative and very useful present.

2 Spread the herbs out in groups on the work surface. It is much easier to work this way rather than to try to disentangle a single stem from a bucketful of herbs.

3 Assemble the posy, holding it loosely in one hand and adding and adjusting with the other.

4 When you are happy with the arrangement, tie firmly around the base of the stems with string.

5 Trim the ends of the stems level and decorate the posy with a ribbon bow.

MATERIALS AND EQUIPMENT
selection of freshly picked herbs
bucket
string
scissors
ribbon

ABOVE: *Any fresh herbs left over from the posy can be hung up in a window to dry. Wrap in paper if you want to retain the flavour for culinary purposes.*

1 Condition the herbs by standing them in deep water in a bucket for at least three hours before making the posy.

SAGE AND TANSY HEART

Like many other herbs, tansy and sage both dry well and are perfect companions. When picked at its prime, tansy will dry maintaining the yellow colouring of the flowers. (See the Chef's Herbs project for the correct way to dry herbs.) For this project, a simple heart shape is formed out of thick garden wire and small bunches of the herbs are wired in place to make a charming and aromatic decorative hanging.

MATERIALS AND EQUIPMENT
pliers
thick, plastic-coated garden wire
fine green florist's wire
30 small bunches of dried sage
12 small bunches of dried tansy
50 cm (20 in) yellow cord

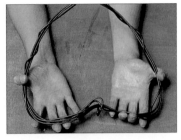

3 Holding the wire circle firmly in both hands with the loop positioned opposite you, carefully bend into a symmetrical heart shape.

1 Using the pliers, make a small loop at the end of the thick wire. Lay the wire on the work surface and form a circle approximately 30 cm (12 in) in diameter. Repeat to make three more rings of wire lying on top of the first circle. Cut off the wire with the pliers.

4 Use the fine green florist's wire to bind the small bunches of herbs neatly and securely.

5 Starting at the top of the heart, wire the bunches of herbs on to the frame. Start with the sage and intersperse each two bunches of sage with one bunch of tansy. Work to the bottom of the heart, then start at the top again to complete the other side.

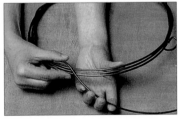

2 Twist the top circle of wire around the other three.

6 To hang the heart, thread the cord through the loop at the top of the heart and tie in a knot.

THE VEGETABLE GARDEN AND ORCHARD

Fruit and vegetable gardening in pots, companion plants and decorative ideas for the productive garden. Enjoy the best the season's harvest has to offer.

Not long ago, virtually every garden had its own vegetable plot and a few fruit trees, and the household relied on the food they provided. The whole family was aware of the passing year as they munched their way through a fairly monotonous diet of root vegetables and brassicas during the winter, joyfully greeted the arrival of spring with its salads and tender young vegetables and helped prepare and preserve the fruit and vegetables from the glut of summer and autumn. Fewer of us now grow fruit and vegetables from economic necessity. For most of us living in developed countries, producing our own food has become a pleasant pastime and an opportunity for healthy exercise, rather than a matter of survival. While we are fortunate that we can take a fairly relaxed attitude towards vegetable production, there is nothing quite like eating home-grown food, and there is also pleasure to be had in the rituals and requirements of the orchard and vegetable plot.

The early winter months are spent perusing seed catalogues and ordering far too many seeds as the optimistic gardener is seduced by the tantalizing photos. There is the occasional foray into the garden on fine, crisp days to tidy up, dig over the vegetable patch and prune fruit trees, but the gardening year proper begins in the potting shed when a space is cleared on the bench to sprout seed potatoes and sow early salads in pots and trays. Soon it is time

Top: Home-grown vegetables seem to have a flavour all their own.

to go out into the spring sunshine to prepare seed beds, transplant seedlings and put pea sticks and bean poles in place. In late spring, the pace hots up as everything starts growing at an enthralling rate and there is plenty to do:

thinning, weeding, watering and trying to outwit the pests which are as intent on a gourmet experience as is the gardener. With late summer and autumn comes the harvest and the opportunity to feast on the fruits of the year's labours with an appreciation and enjoyment that can never be simulated by filling the supermarket trolley.

A small garden need be no obstacle to the would-be vegetable gardener; space can always be found for a few vegetables, whether they are runner beans grown up a decorative plant support or lettuces in the flower bed and tomatoes in pots. Some vegetables are positively decorative and don't look out of place in the herbaceous border: ruby chard looks wonderful, even when it has gone to seed; globe artichokes have an architectural beauty; and

the frilly leaves of oak-leaf lettuces look pretty at the front of the border. Even fruit trees can be accommodated; there are dwarf versions of all the most popular varieties and some grow well in pots. Recently, some of the soft fruits have become available as standards and they are a wonderful addition to the garden.

All successful gardening is a combination of good husbandry and good luck. Even the best gardener can sometimes be confounded by bad weather or pests, but remember that there is always next year.

TOP: A wire basket of fresh plums.

LEFT: The best way of storing onions is to hang them up.

POTS OF POTATOES

Digging potatoes is an exciting business – when done on a small scale. There is no possibility of peeping beforehand to check the size of the crop, just the moment of revelation when the root is lifted to disclose its tally of tubers. While the business of harvesting potatoes is mainly a workaday agricultural matter, in your own garden it is a significant moment of celebration or disappointment.

There is a long tradition of raising early potatoes in pots, where they will grow very happily provided they are planted in a rich compost and are kept well watered throughout the growing season. Real enthusiasts will plant a pot of potatoes in the greenhouse in late autumn to be harvested for eating on Christmas Day. Choose a variety of potato which is recommended for good flavour and firm flesh – one of the salad potatoes would be ideal. To speed up the process, it is normal to allow the tubers to sprout in light before planting, although this is not essential.

It is usually advisable to grow potatoes from certified seed stock grown at high altitude to prevent the possibility of introducing disease, but buying a bag of seed potatoes for one pot is unnecessarily cautious. Three or four neglected tubers sprouting in the vegetable rack will be all you need, or if you are a better housekeeper, stand some of your chosen potatoes in an egg box on the bench of the potting shed until they have started to sprout. Rub off all but two of the sprouts before planting. When you plant the tubers, only half-fill the pot with compost, and as the plants grow and the leaves appear, "earth them up" regularly – this means covering the leaves with another layer of compost. This encourages the plant to grow more roots on which tubers will form and therefore increases the size of the crop.

Be sure to plant a pot of mint at the same time as you plant the potatoes. The two pots will make a delightful gift for a friend, but you are certain to want to plant more to keep for yourself, to experience the bliss of a plate of steamed, freshly dug potatoes and mint.

ABOVE: A pot of newly dug potatoes is complemented by a bunch of fresh mint. When presenting the potato pot as a gift for later harvesting, include a small pot of mint as well.

MATERIALS AND EQUIPMENT
*half barrel or large pot
compost enriched with manure
3–5 potatoes (sprouted for an early crop)
fork or trowel*

1 Fill the base of the barrel or pot with a generous layer of compost (so that it is approximately a quarter full).

2 Arrange the potatoes 15 cm (6 in) apart on the surface of the compost. Cover with another layer of compost until the container is no more than approximately half full.

3 Water thoroughly after planting and continue to water whenever the compost shows any sign of drying out. A weak liquid fertilizer may be applied if manure is not available.

4 When the leaves appear and reach 10 cm (4 in) in height, add another layer of compost to cover them completely. Repeat this process until the pot is full of compost.

5 Continue to water regularly. The plants are ready to harvest once they have flowered.

6 Dig up the plants carefully using a fork or trowel. Only dig up as many potatoes as you need. The others will keep better if they remain in the soil until you want them.

COMPANION PLANTS

Just as the company of convivial friends often brings out the best in us, so certain plants have been observed to grow better in association with others. Sometimes this is because the companion plant secretes substances that deter pests or stimulates the other plant's growth, but sometimes the reason is less obvious – they just seem to do better together than apart, which is surely the definition of a successful relationship! Conversely, one plant can exercise a malign influence on another, and when the two are planted together, one will thrive at the expense of the other – a situation also paralleled in human experience.

The biodynamic system of farming provides the main authority on companion planting. Based on the teachings of Rudolph Steiner, the system promotes a method of horticulture and agriculture which makes use of the mutual influences of living organisms. The ideas have met with wide acceptance among organic farmers and gardeners, who have found companion planting useful in promoting plant health

ABOVE: Parsley will benefit roses and tomatoes. Plant in moist soil in a partially shaded position, and cut the flower stems down to encourage new leaf growth.

LEFT: Chives will allow apple trees to thrive when planted nearby. The chive plant will grow in almost any soil, and in large quantities aids the growth of carrots.

RIGHT: French marigold prevents white fly from attacking tomatoes.

110

ABOVE: Marjoram is a welcome addition to any garden – neighbouring plants will flourish in its company.

RIGHT: Perfect for the orchard or a single fruit tree, southernwood will repel fruit moths.

RIGHT: As an insect repellent, rosemary will be appreciated by visitors to the garden as well as the surrounding plants.

and defeating pests without recourse to chemical sprays and fertilizers.

Some companion planting is pure common sense; for instance, a low-growing, sun-loving plant will not do well if planted among tall plants that keep it in the shade, while it will thrive among other plants of a similar height. Although it is not practical to mention all the benign and malign associations, some of the most widely accepted and best observed are listed below. Give individual plants to friends, with a list of their beneficial properties.

BASIL grows well among tomatoes.

BORAGE and strawberries are good companions.

CARROTS can be protected from carrot fly by planting them with leeks or among strong-smelling herbs such as rosemary or sage.

CHIVES planted in an orchard are believed to help protect the apple trees from scab. When planted in large quantities they also improve the growth of carrots.

DILL is a good plant to grow with cabbages, but when sown with carrots it must not be allowed to flower or it will reduce the crop.

FOXGLOVES stimulate the growth of plants around them.

FRENCH MARIGOLDS (*tagetes*) release a substance into the soil which kills nematodes, and when grown among tomato plants, they will help prevent white fly.

GARLIC planted among roses helps to keep greenfly at bay and is also thought to increase the fragrance of the roses.

MARJORAM has a beneficial effect on surrounding plants.

NASTURTIUMS help combat white fly in the greenhouse and will attract black fly away from broad beans.

PARSLEY is good for roses and tomatoes.

ROSEMARY has the ability to repel insects.

SOUTHERNWOOD is a moth repellent and can be planted near fruit trees to repel fruit moths.

POTTED FRUIT GARDEN

For most of us, owning our own orchard is the stuff of dreams and, in many ways, this dream orchard is the best one of all. It is a place where venerable trees of great character support swings and hammocks for whiling away the hours in dappled sunlight, reading books or simply daydreaming. In the real world, the orchard is more a place of industrious activity than leisure. Few of us have either the space or the time for such a commitment and we must restrict our fruit growing to a more modest scale.

A potted fruit tree is ideal for the small garden and can be surprisingly productive as well as decorative. An apple tree is essential and the "Ballerina" varieties are particularly suitable for growing in pots. Their single stems bear short lateral branches which produce a heavy crop of apples.

A strawberry pot is also an important element of the potted fruit garden, for although strawberries can now be bought all year round, they rarely bear more than a visual resemblance to the sun-warmed fruit, full of flavour and fragrance, which are picked and consumed straight from the plant. A good strawberry pot has a lip inside the upper edge of each hole in the pot. This prevents the compost leaching out of the holes when you water. When watering a strawberry pot, take care that the lower plants receive their fair share of water.

The choice of other fruit for the potted fruit garden should be made according to personal taste. Many soft fruits, such as raspberries, currants and gooseberries are suitable.

Once the pots are planted, add a mulch of smooth stones or gravel which will help retain moisture and absorb heat. It is particularly important that fruit trees are not allowed to dry out at any stage or they will drop their fruit to improve their chances of survival.

PLANTING A STRAWBERRY POT

MATERIALS
terracotta strawberry pot
broken crocks
loam-based compost suitable for long-term planting
strawberry plants
alpine strawberry plants
clear plastic bottle, base removed
gravel

1 Cover the drainage holes in the base of the strawberry pot with a layer of broken crocks. Fill the pot with compost to just below the lowest set of holes.

2 Remove the strawberry plants from their pots and plant them from the inside, gently feeding the foliage through the holes to the outside. Add compost to cover the roots and fill the pot to the next level of holes. Firm the compost down and plant the next layer of plants.

3 Pierce holes in the plastic bottle. Screw on the cap loosely. Turn the bottle upside down and fill with gravel.

ABOVE: Plant a mixture of heavy-cropping strawberry plants and a few alpine strawberries for the finest flavour of all.

4 Place the plastic bottle in the pot so that the open base will stand clear of the compost. Fill the area around the bottle with compost and plant strawberry plants in the top of the pot. Press the compost down firmly.

5 Cover the compost with gravel. The base of the gravel-filled bottle should protrude by about 1 cm (½ in). Water the pot by pouring water into the bottle. The water will trickle down to all the strawberry plants in the pot.

PLANTING FRUIT TREES AND BUSHES

MATERIALS
*terracotta pots, each at least double the
volume of the pot the plant is currently
planted in
broken crocks
composted stable manure
bone meal
dwarf apple trees
raspberries, currants, gooseberries or
other favourite fruits
loam-based compost suitable for long-
term planting
stones, for mulching*

1 Cover the holes in the base of each
pot with a layer of broken crocks.

2 Cover the crocks with a generous
layer of stable manure, if available, and
scatter a handful of bone meal over the
surface. Compound fertilizer may be
substituted for manure if none is
available.

3 Remove the tree or bush from its pot
and place it in the new container. The
soil level should be at the same point on
the tree's stem as it was previously. If
necessary, add some loam-based
compost to lift the root ball to the
correct height. Gently tease loose some
of the roots on the root ball so that they
will quickly establish themselves.

4 Fill around the root ball with compost
and firm into position.

5 Cover the surface of the compost
with a mulch of stones. Keep the plants
well watered at all times. Keep a careful
watch for pests and fungal diseases and
remember that birds love soft fruits.

GROW YOUR OWN WINE KIT

Nothing could be more rewarding than your own grape vines and harvest, and this idea is on the perfect scale for first-time wine-makers. Plant your vines now and you will soon be ready to start producing your own *vin de maison*. This kit has been designed as the perfect present for an oenophile friend. A wooden wine-box (in this case, once home to a pleasing vintage of Chateau Lynch-Bages) is varnished for use as an appropriate container and a teasing inspiration to the would-be wine-maker. Wine merchants often sell these boxes very inexpensively. A suitable variety of grape, available from specialist nurseries, is planted in a pot and packed into the bark-filled box with some empty bottles, a demijohn, new corks and photocopied labels in the shape of vine leaves. If the cane that supports the vine has no cane guard, push one of the corks on to the end of it to ensure that nobody damages their eyes when bending to admire this amusing and unusual gift. The labels are written with planting and cultivation instructions.

MATERIALS AND EQUIPMENT
wooden wine-box
medium-grade sandpaper
varnish
paintbrush
grape vine
terracotta pot
compost
tracing paper
vine leaf
pen
green paper
cutting mat or thick card
stencil knife or scalpel
bark
clean, empty wine bottles, labels removed
new corks
demijohn

1 Rub down any rough edges on the wooden box with sandpaper. Seal the box with a varnish and leave to dry.

2 Plant the grape vine in the terracotta pot, using extra compost as necessary.

3 To make the labels, place the tracing paper on top of the vine leaf and trace around the leaf with a pen. Draw in some of the main veins.

4 Photocopy the tracing to make the required number of labels.

LEFT AND RIGHT: A variation on this gift might include a basket of fresh plums, bottles and recipes for making fruit spirits.

5 Place the photocopies on the cutting mat or thick card and cut round the leaf with a stencil knife or scalpel.

6 Attach one of the labels to the vine with its name on one side and growing instructions on the other. Fill the box with bark and arrange the various components attractively.

FRUIT-PICKING BASKET

Plastic carrier bags can be used for picking fruit, but they lack the elegance of a wooden or woven basket and can tear easily. This slatted basket is stencilled with images of apples and pears and is given an aged appearance with a tinted varnish. It will certainly make the fruit harvest more of an occasion. When the basket is not in use for fruit picking, it can be hung in the potting shed and filled with some of the indispensable bits and pieces for which it is difficult to find a home. It would also look pretty as a storage container in the kitchen.

3 Place the stencil card on the cutting mat or thick card and cut out the stencil with a stencil knife or scalpel.

4 Fix the stencil to the basket in the desired position with masking tape.

MATERIALS AND EQUIPMENT
tracing paper
pencil
stencil card
aerosol glue
cutting mat or thick card
stencil knife or scalpel
wooden basket
masking tape
acrylic paints: green and red
plate
stencil brush
light oak tinted varnish
paintbrush

1 Trace the templates from the back of the book on to tracing paper.

2 Mount the tracings on a piece of stencil card using the aerosol glue.

5 Mix the paint on a plate to the desired shade of green. Apply to the basket with a stencil brush, employing a stippling action.

6 Apply a blush of red paint to one side of the fruit with the stencil brush.

7 Move the stencil to a new position and continue stencilling the fruit to create an even pattern over the basket. Leave to dry completely.

8 Apply a coat of light oak tinted varnish over the whole basket.

DRIED FRUIT DECORATION

The abundance of fruit produced by just one apple or pear tree can sometimes be overwhelming. When you have stored, bottled and frozen as much as you can and still have some left over, you could have a go at drying the fruit. Dried fruit is a delicious and healthy alternative to biscuits and sweets and can also be used decoratively, as in this Shaker-style hanging. Dip the apple and pear slices in fresh rather than bottled lemon juice, as the fresh juice will discolour the fruit less. You might consider making smaller hangings suitable for a Christmas tree.

INGREDIENTS AND EQUIPMENT
apples
pears
sharp knife
fresh lemon juice
wooden skewers
string
cinnamon sticks
raffia
scissors

1 Slice the apples crossways and the pears lengthways with a sharp knife. Make the slices as thin as possible. Dip the slices in lemon juice, then thread them on the wooden skewers, leaving spaces between the slices.

2 Stand to dry in a warm place where air can circulate around the fruit. They are ready when they feel leathery.

3 Lay the dried fruit, string, cinnamon sticks and raffia on the work surface and start assembling the hanging. Form a loop in the end of the string for hanging and tie a cinnamon stick just below the loop. Thread on half a dozen apple slices and tie a large, knobbly knot under the fruit, then add a raffia bow.

ABOVE: Slices of fruit can also be dried slowly in the oven, and hung in a garland across the window. A thick layer of salt will absorb the fruits' juices.

4 Continue building up the decoration until it has reached the desired length. Finish off with a raffia tassel.

THE OUTDOOR ROOM

*Finishing touches and creative projects to give your garden style
and character – practical and decorative candles and holders, pretty
furniture and eye-catching hangings.*

Agarden can fulfil many functions – practical, decorative and pleasurable. During long summer evenings the indoors comes outside as we dine and sit with friends, or simply enjoy the last rays of the setting sun. Make the most of your garden at this time of year, and enjoy embellishing your "outdoor room" with all kinds of personal touches.

Unless your garden is of pocket-handkerchief size, which would dictate that it ought to be treated as a whole, your "outdoor room" should be in some way separated from the rest of the garden. The separation can be quite subtle – a simple change of ground covering from lawn to paving, for example

– or it can be a positive statement with hedges, trellis or fencing. Keep the practicalities in mind. It should be near the house for convenience and it should be accessible via a hard surface so that you avoid muddy shoes when the grass is wet. Unless you are blessed with a hot climate, it should benefit from full sun for at least part of the day and should be pleasantly sheltered. However beautiful the view, an outdoor room in a position which catches the prevailing wind will only be used on the stillest of days. It is better to find a sheltered

ABOVE RIGHT: Unusual planters add visual interest.

LEFT: Sunflowers can be grown in beds, or to hide an unsightly wall.

122

corner for your room and restrict yourself to a bench from which to admire the view.

Once you have chosen the site for your room, you can set about furnishing it. You will certainly need some larger pieces of furniture such as tables and chairs for *al fresco* meals. In the quest for style and beauty in the outdoor room do not abandon comfort. It is a sad fact that some of the most attractive garden chairs are excruciatingly uncomfortable – always try out chairs before buying, and imagine yourself sitting in that position for an hour. A surprising number fail this test.

Now that we are all so much more conscious of the harm that the sun can do us, it is important to provide shade, especially over the table and surrounding chairs. A large parasol is the most flexible and adaptable way of doing this as it can also function to keep the diners dry in sudden downpours. On hot days a terrace or patio can become very warm indeed, especially when south-facing – to lower the temperature, use a trick from the greenhouse and water the paving with a hose or watering can and the air will immediately become pleasantly cool.

Finishing touches will add character to the room; lighting for the evenings, something to hang on the walls, table coverings and decorative objects to draw the eye. For real individuality, the addition of a few accessories made or decorated by yourself will do much to impart your own style.

Top: A bird table is very simple to construct, and will draw flocks of birds to the garden.

Above right: A weathered sundial nestling amongst the greenery.

CUSTOMIZED NESTING BOX

Ready-made nesting boxes are available in every shape and size – they range from modest to palatial dwellings and are generally priced accordingly. If the birds in your garden are upwardly mobile (and aren't they all!) but your pocket isn't, a simple, inexpensive birdhouse can be transformed with a lick of paint and a few decorative touches. The Shaker-style paintwork on this birdhouse uses leftover paint, the finial is cut from scrap timber and the perch is an apple twig. If your birds might prefer a more metropolitan dwelling, paint the nesting box blue-grey and roof it with some copper foil left over from the Romantic Lily Candles project. The door surround is also made from the copper foil. Remember to bend the foil back on itself rather than lining the hole or the birds may injure themselves on the sharp edges. To ensure that the nesting box gives you maximum pleasure, position it so it can be seen from both the outdoor room and the house. To give the birds maximum pleasure and security, hang the nesting box well out of reach of cats and other predators and where overhanging foliage will provide some shelter and privacy.

LEFT: An alternative decoration using copper foil.

2 Draw the door and heart motifs with the permanent marker pen.

3 Fill in the design and the finial with the second colour of emulsion paint and leave to dry completely.

4 Glue the finial in place at the front of the roof ridge using PVA glue.

MATERIALS AND EQUIPMENT
nesting box
emulsion paint in 2 colours
paintbrush
permanent marker pen
decorative finial cut from a piece of
scrap pine
PVA glue
drill
apple twig

1 Paint the box with the first colour of emulsion paint and leave to dry.

5 Drill a hole of the same diameter as the apple twig beneath the entrance hole. Apply a little glue to the twig and push it in position.

124

EARTHY PAINTED POTS

Liquid seaweed plant food is a wonderful rich brown colour and when diluted can be painted on to terracotta pots to give the appearance of ageing. It will also encourage the growth of algae. Undiluted, the colour is very deep and looks beautiful when used to decorate pots. To keep the colours as rich as they are when first applied, you will need to seal the surface with a matt varnish. Alternatively, leave the pots unsealed – most of the coating will quickly wash away if the pots get wet and the resulting soft patterning will look rather like faded frescoes.

MATERIALS AND EQUIPMENT
masking tape
terracotta pots
liquid seaweed plant food
paintbrushes
matt varnish (optional)

2 Apply the liquid seaweed plant food to the unpainted areas with a small paintbrush and leave to dry fully.

3 Carefully peel off the masking tape and seal the whole pot with a coat of matt varnish if required.

1 Use masking tape to protect the areas of the pot that you want to remain unpainted.

BELOW: Here, terracotta has been painted a grey-green, with soft pink stripes to complement the plant.

WEATHERED GARDEN FURNITURE

When looking around antique shops which specialize in old garden furniture, it can be quite shocking to see the prices charged for these items. Simple folding chairs, once used in their thousands in municipal parks, are now desirable objects with their faded paintwork and weathered wood, and they fetch premium prices. A far less expensive alternative is to buy hardwood folding chairs from a DIY store and do a bit of instant weathering yourself. Four chairs transformed in this way will cost about the same as one antique chair. To achieve the weathered effect, the chair is first sanded down, then randomly rubbed over with a household candle before being painted. The paint should be applied in a slapdash way; make no attempt to get into all the corners or achieve an even coating. Once the paint is dry, the chair is rubbed down with wire wool to remove any paint from the waxed areas. When the chair is left out in the garden, nature will continue the weathering process, and within a season you will have your own set of heirlooms.

MATERIALS AND EQUIPMENT
folding wooden garden chair
medium-grade sandpaper
household candle
one-coat white emulsion paint
paintbrush
wire wool

1 Rub down the surface of the chair with sandpaper to make a better key for the paint.

2 Rub over the surface randomly with the candle, applying the wax thickly on the corners and edges.

3 Paint the chair with white emulsion paint using random brush strokes and leave to dry completely.

4 Rub down the paintwork with the wire wool to remove the paint from the waxed areas.

ABOVE: A similar technique was applied to this wheelbarrow, which has been used to display trugs of violas.

CITRONELLA CANDLES

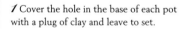

The pleasure of a summer evening in the garden, sitting around the table for an *al fresco* meal, can be considerably diminished by the presence of biting insects intent on their own feast. Candles scented with essential oils which have insect-repellent properties will provide soft light and see off the enemy. Citronella oil is the most commonly used and is agreed to be the most effective, but some people dislike the scent and lavender, peppermint or a mixture of geranium and eucalyptus can be used instead. On evenings when insects are a particular problem, burn some undiluted oil in an oil burner to encourage the insects to leave before you sit down to eat. The candles will then continue the good work, as well as perfuming the air. Materials for candle-making are available from craft shops or by mail order (see the Suppliers list at the back of the book). Self-hardening clay is available from art shops.

MATERIALS AND EQUIPMENT
2 7.5 cm (3 in) old terracotta pots
self-hardening clay
175 g (6 oz) paraffin wax
50 g (2 oz) natural beeswax
heatproof bowl
double boiler
2 15 cm (6 in) wicks suitable for
candles 7.5 cm (3 in) in diameter
2 short lengths of wooden skewer
50 drops citronella essential oil
spoon
scissors

1 Cover the hole in the base of each pot with a plug of clay and leave to set.

2 Place the waxes in the heatproof bowl and melt in a double boiler.

3 Dip the lengths of wick into the wax and leave for a few minutes to harden.

4 Return the bowl of wax to the double boiler to prevent it from setting.

BELOW: Small terracotta pots make appropriate candle holders for the garden. Make sure the candles are firmly fixed into the bases of the pots.

5 Rest the skewers across the pots. Position each wick to hang centrally in the pot and fold the end over.

6 Add the essential oil to the wax and stir well to mix.

7 Pour the wax into the pots to just below the rim. Tap the sides to release any air bubbles. Keep back a little wax.

8 As the candles cool, a dip will form around the wick. Fill this with the remaining wax. Trim the wick.

WARNING
It is essential that the waxes are melted in a double boiler as they are highly flammable.

STAY-PUT PICNIC CLOTH

Most of us have experienced the irritation caused by a blow-away cloth which lifts itself from the ground or the table on which it has been spread, then drops into a beetroot salad to become permanently stained and knocks over a couple of glasses of wine. In the ensuing chaos, we resolve to restrict meals to the dining room in future. A happier solution to the problem is a weighted cloth that cannot be dislodged by a sudden breeze. Circular metal curtain weights are slipped into the folds at each corner of the cloth and held in place with Velcro. These will keep the cloth firmly in place when in use and can quickly and easily be removed before laundering.

MATERIALS AND EQUIPMENT
2m (2 yd) of 1.5 m (59 in) wide fabric
dressmaker's scissors
iron
tape measure
sewing machine or needle
sewing thread
15 cm (6 in) heavy-duty Velcro or 4 Velcro discs
4 circular metal curtain weights

1 Fold the fabric diagonally across itself to make a triangle. Cut the fabric along the edge of the triangle to make a square. The offcut can be used to make matching napkins.

2 Open out the fabric, which will now be a perfect square. Fold over all four edges by 2.5 cm (1 in) and press in place with a hot iron.

3 Fold over the corners of the cloth to make triangles 8 cm (3¼ in) high, and press in place.

4 Fold over a further 6 cm (2¼ in) around the edges and press. The corners will now meet in a fold.

5 Stitch all around the cloth 6 mm (¼ in) from the edge and again 6 mm (¼ in) inside the edge of the hem.

6 Remove the adhesive backing from a small piece of Velcro or a Velcro disc, insert into one of the corner folds and stick in place. Attach the opposite piece of Velcro onto one of the curtain weights. When using the cloth, simply slip the weights into position and the Velcro will hold them in place.

LEFT: The weighted cloth is so easy to make, you will want to make several to suit the colours of the season.

ROMANTIC LILY CANDLES

The romantic effect of flickering candlelight on the night-time garden has long been appreciated. In the sixteenth and seventeenth centuries, some of the great London parks were known as "pleasure gardens", and with avenues of trees hung with thousands of candles in coloured glass holders, they were the venue for much dalliance and delight. Today, most garden lighting consists of the harsh glare of security lights, good for keeping burglars at bay but not conducive to gazing up at the night sky. More subtle outdoor lighting is available and is becoming more sophisticated, but at a price which would douse the ardour of most latter-day

Cyranos. Impoverished lovers need not despair, for magical effects can be created using empty jam jars and sheets of copper foil. The materials may sound prosaic but the results are not. The copper foil is soft enough to cut with scissors but firm enough not to be fragile. A pattern is impressed into the soft foil and holes pierced through it with a bradawl. The panel is then wrapped around the outside of a jam jar and held in place with paper fasteners. To make the jar into a lantern, wrap copper wire around the neck and attach a hanging loop. Copper foil is available by mail order (see the Suppliers list at the back of the book).

MATERIALS AND EQUIPMENT
glass jars in varying sizes
ruler
0.005 (36 gauge) copper foil
scissors
felt-tip pen
tracing paper
newspaper
ballpoint pen
bradawl
brass paper fasteners
candles

1 Measure the height of each jar from just above the base to just below the neck. For each jar, cut a panel from the copper foil of the measured height and long enough to wrap around the jar with a 1 cm (½ in) overlap.

2 Use the felt-tip pen to trace the lily template from the back of the book on to tracing paper.

3 Place the foil panel on a wad of folded newspaper and place the tracing on top. Firmly outline the lily design using the ballpoint pen.

4 Remove the tracing paper and pierce the pattern of dots on the petals using the bradawl and making the holes of even size.

WARNING
Handle cut copper foil with caution. It can sometimes produce fine slivers of foil if it is not cut cleanly.

5 Wrap the panel around the jar and mark the fastening points where the foil overlaps. Pierce these with the bradawl and make the panel into a cylinder using the paper fasteners.

6 Slip the foil cylinder over the jar and stand a candle inside.

BELOW: *Paper bags perforated with a pattern of holes make pretty outdoor lanterns for short-term use. Fill the bottom with sand and place a night-light inside. Do not leave unattended at any time.*

WIND CHIMES

A walk on the beach or in the woods to gather weathered twigs and a forage around the potting shed will provide you with all the materials for these rustic wind chimes. The bells are made from miniature terracotta pots with metal vine-eyes as clappers. Provided the pots have no cracks, the wind chimes will sound like distant cow-bells to add a third sensual dimension to the visual and fragrant delights of your outdoor room.

MATERIALS AND EQUIPMENT
110 cm (44 in) galvanized wire
wire cutters
4 weathered twigs of different sizes, the largest 30 cm (12 in) long
drill
3 corks
2 vine-eyes
5 cm (2 in) old terracotta pots

1 Cut the wire into one 50 cm (20 in) length and two 30 cm (12 in) lengths using wire cutters. Make a hanging loop at one end of the 50 cm (20 in) length.

2 Twist the wire around the centre of the longest twig. Drill a hole through the centre of each of the corks and thread one on to the wire.

3 Add the next twig, either by twisting the wire around it as before, or by drilling a hole through the centre and threading it on.

4 Add a second cork, followed by the third twig and the third cork.

BELOW: *Alternative materials for wind chimes could include shells and sand dollars threaded with raffia.*

5 Make a hook from the remaining length of wire and trim if necessary. Drill a hole through one end of the final twig and hook it on to the wire.

6 Thread a vine-eye on to each of the two 30 cm (12 in) lengths of wire and bend over 2.5 cm (1 in) of the wire so that it lies flat against the vine-eye. Wrap the other end of the wire around the vine-eye in a spiral.

7 Thread each vine-eye through the hole in one of the terracotta pots, so that the wide end of the vine-eye becomes the clapper and the narrow end protrudes from the pot.

8 Hang up the wind chimes and attach the bells, making sure that the wind chimes balance. Twist the wires protruding from the bells securely around the twig.

PAINTED PEAT POTS

In most gardens, any peat pots not used up by late spring tend to hang around the shed getting trodden on and battered until they are of little use for next year's seeds. Rather than abandoning them to this ignominious fate, you could be practical and tidy them away or, more interestingly, give them a paint finish and use them as "tidies" for some of the bits and pieces lying around the potting shed. Painted in a terracotta colour mixed from leftover pots of paint and with a dusting of white paint, they resemble old terracotta pots, which often develop a bloom of white salts.

MATERIALS AND EQUIPMENT
acrylic or emulsion paints,
including white
paintbrushes
peat pots
card

1 Mix a terracotta colour of paint and apply to the peat pots. Leave to dry.

2 Dip a clean paintbrush into white paint, then remove most of the paint from the brush by dabbing it on to a piece of card. When the brush is barely coated and quite dry, apply the paint lightly and patchily to the peat pots.

BELOW: *The paint finish brings out the texture of the peat pots as they serve a new function as containers for odds and ends.*

MOSS AND NETTING URNS

⟨✦⟩

This project provides the opportunity for some real potting shed magic – disappear into your shed with a length of chicken wire, some plastic pots and a bag of moss and emerge half an hour later with a collection of beautiful urns that can be used as garden decorations for a special occasion. When not in use, keep the urns in a dark corner of the shed to preserve the colour of the moss, which fades quite quickly in daylight. Made without the moss lining, the urns become quirky sculptures useful as decorative containers for lightweight objects. Moss is available in bags from garden centres and sheets of dried moss can also be bought from dried flower stockists.

MATERIALS AND EQUIPMENT
chicken wire
wire cutters
moss
florist's reel wire
20 cm (8 in) plastic pot

1 Cut a 1.5 m (59 in) length of chicken wire. Fold it in half so the raw edges meet and pack a layer of moss between the layers of wire.

2 Fold the chicken wire and moss "sandwich" in half lengthways and join the edges securely together with lengths of florist's reel wire.

4 Leave the pot in place and firmly squeeze the chicken wire with both hands just below the pot to make the neck of the urn.

3 Slip the plastic pot into the top end (the one with no rough edges) and form the lip of the urn by folding the chicken wire outwards from the rim of the pot.

5 Make the base of the urn by folding the rough edges inwards and squeezing and squashing the wire until it has taken the desired shape. Keep standing the urn on its base as you work to check that it is level, and adjust as necessary.

LEFT: Whether the moss is fresh, as here, or has been allowed to dry out, the container has a pleasingly textural quality.

RIGHT: Unadorned, the wire shape alone makes a striking container.

BIRD-LOVER'S GIFT BOX

Urban and suburban gardens are havens for wild birds, especially if the gardener is in the habit of regularly putting out food and fresh water. The birds soon get to know and will pass the word around to make your bird table a regular stopping-off point. There is immense pleasure to be had from knowing that you are helping the wild bird population to thrive and from watching the number of species which come to feed daily. A gift box containing a simple bird table and a variety of bird food can be the start of an engrossing hobby for a friend. The bird table is made from two pieces of rough timber nailed together with battens to strengthen the table and with a lip around the edge to stop nuts and seeds rolling off. String is tied to a hook in each corner so that the table can be hung in a tree, out of reach of predators. To complete the gift box, roll plastic pots diagonally in squares of brown paper to form cones and add some different types of bird food. Recipes for additional bird treats can also be included, or a decorative container to hold water.

MATERIALS AND EQUIPMENT
rough timber, 25 x 13 x 1 cm (10 x 5 x ½ in) (x 2)
battens, 25 x 2.5 x 2.5 cm (10 x 1 x 1 in) (x 2)
and 28 x 5 x 1 cm (11 x 2 x ½ in) (x 4)
nails
hammer
wood preservative
paintbrush
4 brass hooks
2 m (2 yd) sisal string
scissors

1 Join together the two pieces of rough timber by positioning them side by side and placing the two 25 cm (10 in) battens across the wood, one at each end. Nail the battens securely in place to make the base.

2 Nail the four 28 cm (11 in) lengths of batten around the edges of the flat side of the table, allowing a lip of at least 2.5 cm (1 in).

3 Paint all the surfaces of the table with wood preservative and leave to dry.

4 Screw a brass hook into each corner of the table.

5 Cut the sisal string into four equal lengths and tie a small loop in one end of each piece. Attach each loop to a hook, then gather up the strings above the table and tie in a loop for hanging.

LEFT: Pots containing different varieties of bird seed complete the gift, packed in a wooden basket. Specialist bird seed manufacturers are able to provide information on which types of seed attract particular species of bird.

142

MOSAIC HEARTS

Most gardens are a source of treasure, however modest it might be. As we turn the soil, broken and weathered pieces of china and glass are uncovered and, if they are saved, they can be used to make decorative mosaics for the outdoor room. There is a real sense of satisfaction to be gained from turning a previous gardener's discarded rubbish into something attractive. Pieces of weathered green glass set in tile cement are used to make these pretty hearts, which are moulded in biscuit cutters. Hang them on a wall or fence, or simply set them within a rock garden.

MATERIALS AND EQUIPMENT
heart-shaped biscuit cutter
petroleum jelly
green garden wire
scissors
thick card
ready-mixed tile cement
bowl of water
weathered pieces of glass (or china)

1 Coat the biscuit cutter with petroleum jelly to make removing the finished mosaic easier.

2 Cut a short length of wire and make it into a loop. Position the loop at the top of the heart with the end of the wire bent up inside the mould.

BELOW: Larger-scale mosaic projects might include this quirky design.

3 Place the mould on the card and half fill with tile cement. Smooth the surface of the cement with wet fingers.

4 Arrange the pieces of glass or china on the surface of the cement. If a piece needs to be repositioned, wash it under the tap to clean it before reusing.

5 Leave the mosaic to dry for 24 hours or until it feels solid to the touch. Gently remove it from the mould.

METALLIC-EFFECT BUCKETS

The luminous, blue-green tones of verdigris and the burnished hues of gold and bronze always complement plants, and the effects are not difficult to reproduce on cheap, galvanized buckets.

MATERIALS AND EQUIPMENT
galvanized buckets
medium-grade sandpaper
metal primer
small and large paintbrushes
acrylic paints: gold, white, aqua
and rust
amber shellac
natural sponge
polyurethane varnish

1 Sand the buckets, then prime with metal primer. Allow to dry for two to three hours. Paint with gold paint and allow to dry for two to three hours.

2 Paint with amber shellac and allow to dry for 30 minutes. For the verdigris effect, mix white acrylic paint with aqua and dilute with water. For a rusted effect, mix white acrylic paint with rust-coloured paint and dilute as before.

3 Sponge the verdigris paint on to one bucket, and the rust paint on to the other, allowing some of the gold to show through. Leave to dry for one to two hours. Apply a coat of varnish.

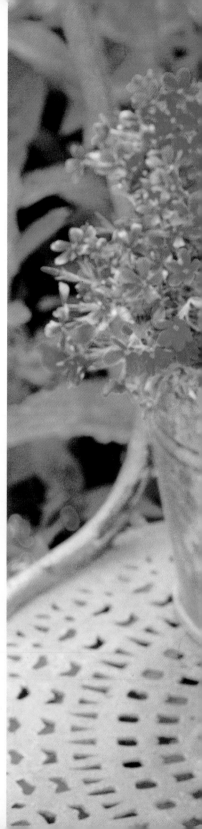

SEASONAL CHECKLIST

While it is by no means comprehensive, this list will provide some guidance to the major tasks in the garden and potting shed and when they are best carried out.

MID-WINTER

With little to do in the garden, this is the time for tidying up the shed. Sort the pots and seed trays into sizes and stack accordingly. Put away all the bits and pieces still lying around on the bench and make a list of all the things you are running out of: string, raffia, plant rings, etc. Check your tools and see which need repair or replacement. Replenish your first aid kit. Feed the birds and put out a regular supply of water in freezing weather.

LATE WINTER

On fine days, go out into the garden and tidy up any dead stalks and leaves that you didn't deal with in the autumn, before the new growth starts. Prune fruit trees and bushes on frost-free days. Turn the soil in the vegetable garden in dry weather. Sow early vegetable seeds. Check the nesting boxes are in good order. Continue to feed the birds.

EARLY SPRING

Now is the time for action. In the shed, sow seeds in pots and seed trays and set seed potatoes to sprout. Outdoors, prepare seed beds in the vegetable garden, plant out early vegetables sown in late winter under cover, and sow more seeds. Prune and feed the roses in fine weather. Tidy pots in the outdoor room and elsewhere in the garden and top up with compost. Divide large clumps of herbs such as chives, mint and marjoram and replant or pot up to give away. At the first sign of baby birds hatching, stop feeding the birds. The nuts and seeds eaten by the adults are not suitable for the babies.

SPRING

Once the weather has warmed up, the weeds start growing faster than the young seedlings. Regular weeding now will save work later in the year and will stop the weeds from robbing the young plants of vital nutrients. Check that pea and bean supports are still in good order

and are ready to use. Put plant supports in the borders while the plants are still quite small – this is much easier than when they start to spread and lean. Replace plant saucers under outdoor pots. As potted bulbs finish flowering, move them to a position where they can die down undisturbed. Tulip bulbs should be lifted once they have fully died back and stored in sacks.

LATE SPRING

Plant out tender plants once the risk of frost has passed and keep up with the weeding. Pick early herbs and vegetables. Plant up summer displays in pots, hanging baskets and borders. Pot up leftover young plants and give them to friends.

EARLY SUMMER

This is the time when the garden is at its loveliest, so make time to appreciate it and also go out to visit other gardens for pleasure and inspiration. Photograph flowers when they are at their best to use on home-made seed packets. Cut flowers for the house and herbs and vegetables for the kitchen. Cut flowers and herbs for drying. Keep weeding and water and feed pot plants regularly. Deadhead roses as necessary. Keep a look-out for pest infestations and treat promptly. Soft fruit will be ripening, so protect from the birds and pick when ready. Make garden candle holders for warm evenings.

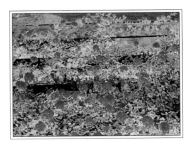

MID-SUMMER

The weeds will now be slowing down as the plants take up more space, so use the extra time to concentrate on regular deadheading and watering to keep things looking their best. Continue to photograph the flowers for seed packets. Eat outdoors as often as possible, and make a weighted tablecloth for breezier evenings. Pick and preserve fruit and vegetables to enjoy in winter.

LATE SUMMER

This is a quieter month in the garden as plants mature and growth slows. Gather seed as it matures on flower stems and place the stems in paper bags to hang up in the shed to dry fully. If you are going away on holiday, move pots into a shady corner and cut back the growth on annuals and tender perennials, which will grow and flower with renewed vigour after this treatment. Ask a friend to check the garden and water as necessary while you are away, to avoid disappointment on your return.

EARLY AUTUMN

By now, the potting shed is probably looking fairly chaotic. Tidy it up before you start taking cuttings and bringing tender plants indoors to be potted up and cut back to keep over the winter. Gather seed from late-flowering plants. Harvest main-crop vegetables and orchard fruit and store surplus for use during the coming months. Do not store apples and potatoes together as they taint one another. Apples should be laid on slatted shelves, not touching and in a cool, dark, airy place. Potatoes and other root crops should be stored buried in peat or sand. Move a small quantity into sacks as you are ready to use them. Onions, garlic and shallots can be hung from the rafters until needed. Plant out brassicas. Take cuttings of shrubs and tender plants.

AUTUMN

Continue harvesting and storing. Cut back frosted or dying growth in the borders and mulch with compost. As the vegetable garden is cleared, dig over the beds. Remove pea and bean sticks and bundle up ready for next year. Plant spring bulbs in the garden and in pots. Move decorative plant supports, garden furniture and delicate terracotta under cover and repair before storing.

LATE AUTUMN

Remove plant saucers from under terracotta pots – if the saucers fill up with water which then freezes and so expands, the pots are more likely to get damaged during the winter. Make up seed packets and fill with seeds stored in the shed.

WINTER

Make the occasional foray to the potting shed to do something quietly creative. Check the seed packets from last year, throw away any that are out-of-date and make a note of what is needed. Peruse the seed catalogues and order the plants of your dreams.

TECHNIQUES

COLLECTING SEEDS

When you are tidying the garden, resist the temptation to cut down every flowering stem that is past its best. Leave a few and allow the seed to ripen on the plant. The seed is usually ready for collection when you can hear it rattling inside the seed pod and the stem has started to go brown and dry. On a dry day, cut the stems in short lengths and place them in brown paper bags marked with the variety and date of collection. Tie the neck of the bags with string and hang them up to dry in the potting shed.

STORING SEEDS

Leave seeds collected and hung in the shed until autumn, then take the bags down and shake them vigorously to loosen most of the seeds. Open the bags and empty the seeds on to a sheet of paper. Remove bits of dead foliage and twigs and decant the seeds into a prepared packet. Seal and mark with the

RIGHT: Dried seeds are poured on to brown paper before packaging and labelling.

SOWING SEEDS

1 Fill the pot with compost, then level the surface. Firm lightly, but do not pack down the compost.

2 Large seeds should be positioned individually. Make holes in the compost with a pencil or stick.

3 Cover the seeds with another layer of compost, sifting gently to ensure an even distribution. Firm the top again.

name and the date of collection. Seed should be stored in a cool, dry place in a box with a close-fitting lid. Purchased seed will be stamped with a use-by date and is unlikely to germinate consistently after that date, although seed sold in foil packets will stay fresh until the packet is opened.

SOWING SEEDS

Seeds are best sown in a specially formulated seed and cutting compost in clean pots or seed trays. Read the instructions on the packet. Some seeds need special treatment to germinate but most will grow quite easily. Fill the tray or pot with compost to within 2 cm (¾ in) of the rim. Level the surface and firm lightly with a pot or piece of wood. Scatter small seeds thinly over the surface and position large seeds individually; with really big seeds, make holes in the compost with a dibber or pencil and drop in the seeds. Cover with a thin layer of compost and firm lightly again. Water with a fine rose on the watering can, cover with a sheet of glass and place in the dark in a warm position until germination takes place, then move into the light. Transplant when the secondary leaves are well developed and the seedlings are growing strongly. Some seedlings are slow to grow and liquid feed may be necessary as proprietary composts only contain sufficient food for six weeks' growth.

TRANSPLANTING

When transplanting a seedling into another pot, don't be tempted to move straight on to a large pot so that you can skip a process. Seedlings seldom thrive in these conditions. When transplanting to outdoors, leave the plants outside in their pots for a few days to "harden off" before you plant them in the garden. Do your outdoor transplanting in the cool of the evening and water well. The young

ABOVE: After drying in paper cones to preserve their flavour, herbs intended for culinary use can be stored in jars or containers with close-fitting lids. The leaves should be removed from the stems first.

plants will then have the night and early morning to recover before being exposed to the full sun. With few exceptions, plants should be transplanted so that the soil is at the same level on the stem as it was previously.

DRYING HERBS

The best time to dry most herbs is when they are in full growth but before they have flowered. Regular cutting of herbs from late spring onwards will encourage the production of new stems. Cut the herbs in the morning after any dew has evaporated but before midday. At this time the volatile oils are at their most concentrated and their flavour will be at its best. After midday the oils begin to evaporate into the surrounding air, which is why herbs smell their most fragrant in the afternoon and early evening. Tie the herbs into small bundles and roll them in cones of brown paper. Hang up the herbs to dry in a place with a dry atmosphere and good air circulation. The herbs should be fully dry in three to four weeks. Remove them from the cones. If the herbs are to be used for cooking, store the leaves in dark glass jars with snug-fitting lids. If they are for use in dried flower arrangements, pack the stems into cardboard boxes and store in a warm, dry place until you are ready to use.

TRANSPLANTING SEEDLINGS

1 If more than one seedling is growing, remove from the pot and carefully separate the roots.

2 Replant the seedling into a pot only slightly larger than the original one.

TEMPLATES

Many of the templates below are reproduced actual size so they can be traced straight from the page. To transfer the design, rub over the back of the tracing with a soft pencil. Place the tracing, right-side up, against the surface and draw over the traced lines with a hard pencil. Some of the templates need enlarging. This may be done on a photocopier, or by using a grid system. To do this, draw a grid of evenly spaced squares over the template. On a second sheet of paper, draw a grid with squares twice the size of the previous ones (or whatever proportions you wish) and copy the design, square by square, on to the second grid. Finally, draw over the lines to make sure they are continuous, and transfer on to the desired surface by rubbing the back with a soft pencil as before.

18 cm/7 ¹/₄ in

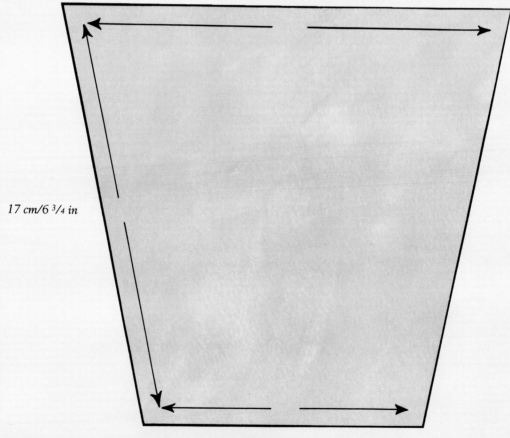

17 cm/6 ³/₄ in

12 cm/5 in

GARDENER'S APRON (TOP POCKET)

25 cm/10 in

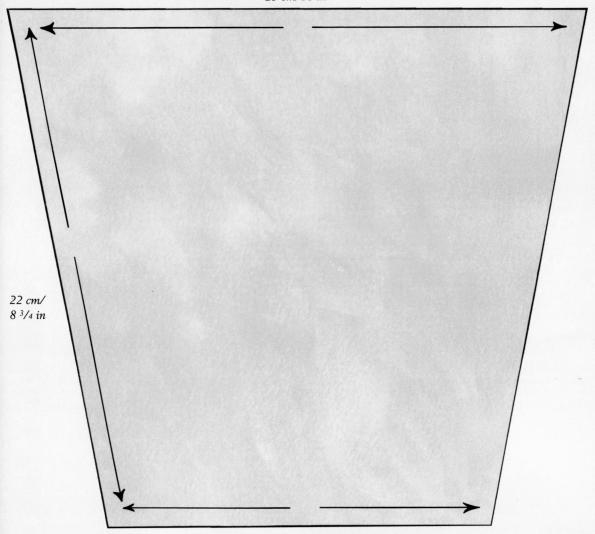

*22 cm/
8 ³/₄ in*

16 cm/6 ¹/₂ in

Gardener's Apron (Bottom Pocket x 2)

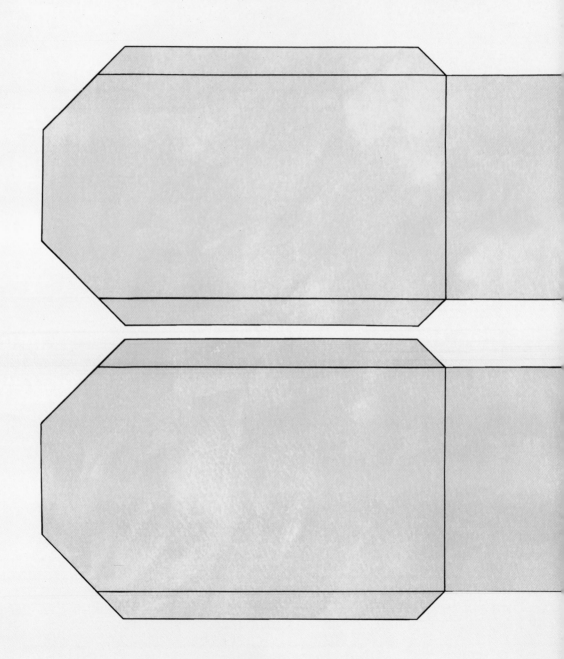

Seed Packets (Reproduced 75%)

Romantic Lily Candles (Reproduced 75%)

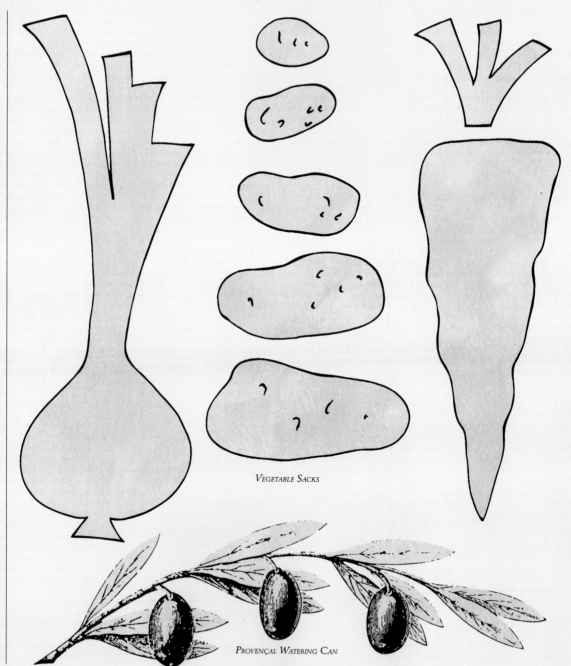

Vegetable Sacks

Provençal Watering Can

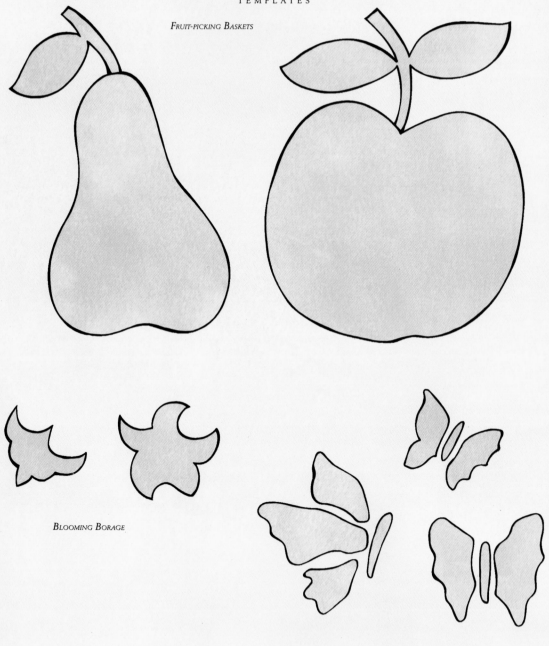

Fruit-picking Baskets

Blooming Borage

Box of Butterflies

157

SUPPLIERS

UNITED KINGDOM

Candle Maker Supplies
28 Blythe Road
London W14 0HA
Tel: 0171 981 5157
Candle-making equipment available by
mail order

Hambleden Herbs
Court Farm
Milverton
Somerset TA4 1NF
Tel: 01823 401205
Dried medicinal and culinary herbs
available by mail order

Harehope Forge Pottery
Harehope Farm
Eglingham
Alnwick
Northumberland
Tel: 01668 217347
Terracotta strawberry pots

The Hop Shop
Castle Farm
Shoreham
Sevenoaks
Kent TN14 7UB
Tel: 01959 523219
Dried flowers and herbs available by
mail order

The Natural Fabric Company
Tel: 01488 684002
Hessian available by mail order

Sussex Trugs Ltd
Herstmonceaux
East Sussex BN27 4LH
Tel: 01323 832137
Traditional trugs

Alec Tiranti
Tel: 0118 930 2775
Copper foil available by mail order

AUSTRALIA

Elegant Garden World Pty Ltd
73-75 Market Street
Condell Park, NSW 2200
Tel: (02) 708 5079
Pots, planters, birdbaths etc

The Parterre Garden
33 Ocean Street
Woollahra, NSW 2025
Tel: (02) 363 5874
New and antique urns

Porter's Original Paints
895 Bourke Street
Waterloo, NSW 2017
Tel: (02) 698 5322
Manufacturers of fine paints

CANADA

Cruikshanks Mail Order
Tel: 1-800-655-5605
Gardening supplies and accessories

PICTURE CREDITS

All photographs are by Michelle
Garrett, except as noted:
Debbie Patterson: pp50 top right,
82 bottom left, 83 top left, 127
bottom, 128 right, 132 bottom left,
144 bottom right (mosaic design by
Cleo Mussi), 146 and 147 (project
by Liz Wagstaff)
Peter Williams: pp58 and 59
(project by Mary Maguire)

ACKNOWLEDGEMENTS

The plants for the spring and autumn
Seasonal Gift Boxes and Baskets were
loaned by Vanstone Park Nursery,
Hitchin Road, Codicote SG4 8TH; tel:
01438 820412.

The peat pots were supplied by Erin
Pots; tel: 01462 475000.

Thanks to Michelle Garrett for her
wonderful photography and the pleasure
of her company, Chris Stainsby for the
use of his delightful garden and Anna
Grant for the wire hanging on page 54.

INDEX

NOTES

NOTES

NOTES

NOTES

NOTES

NOTES

NOTES

NOTES